THE LETTERS
of
ANNE GILCHRIST
and
WALT WHITMAN

By

WALT WHITMAN

Edited with an introduction by

THOMAS B. HARNED

First published in 1918

British Library Cataloguing-in-Publication Data
A catalogue record for this book is available
from the British Library

In Memoriam

AUGUSTA TRAUBEL HARNED

1856-1914

CONTENTS

WALT WHITMAN

Walt Whitman was born on 31st May 1819 in the Town of Huntington, Long Island, New York, USA. He was the second of nine children of Walter Whitman and Louisa Van Velsor Whitman. In part due to a series of bad investments, the family lived in various homes in the Brooklyn area, and Whitman recalled his childhood as generally restless and unhappy, given his family's difficult economic status. Whitman finished his formal schooling at age eleven, and immediately sought employment to aid his family. He worked in an office of a legal firm and later as an apprentice and printer's devil for the weekly Long Island newspaper, the *Patriot*. The following summer, Whitman took a job with the leading Whig newspaper the *Long-Island Star*, and it was here that he developed a strong interest in reading, writing and theatre. He also anonymously published some of his earliest poetry in the *New York Mirror*.

After a brief sojourn as a teacher, living back with his family in Long Island, Whitman returned to New York to establish his own newspaper; the *Long Islander*. He embarked on this project in the spring of 1838, but sold the paper to E.O. Crowell after only ten months. From 1840-41 Whitman attempted to further his career in teaching, but with little success, he returned to writing. During this time, Whitman published a series of ten editorials, called *Sun-Down Papers—From the Desk of a Schoolmaster*, in three newspapers between the winter of 1840 and July 1841. In these essays, he adopted a constructed persona, a technique he would employ throughout his career. It was not until 1850 that Whitman began writing what would later become *Leaves of Grass;* a collection of poetry which he continued editing and revising until his death. The first edition was a success, and stirred up significant interest, partly due to the praise it received by Ralph Waldo Emerson. However the volume, which Whitman intended as 'a distinctly American epic', attracted substantial criticism for its 'offensive' and 'crude' sexual themes. It deviated from the historic use of an elevated hero and instead assumed the identity of the common person; part of the transition in American literature, moving away from transcendentalism towards realism. In light of the contemporary criticism, Whitman's sexuality is often discussed alongside his poetry. Though biographers continue to debate his sexuality, he is usually described as either homosexual or bisexual - yet this remains speculation.

Whitman lived through the American Civil war, and volunteered as a nurse in army hospital, later serving as a clerk in the *Bureau of Indian Affairs* in the Department of the Interior. In June of 1865, Whitman was fired from his job – most likely on moral grounds, by the former Iowa Senator James Harlan, after he found an 1860 edition of *Leaves of Grass*. Whitman's friend William Douglas O'Connor, a well-connected poet and newspaper editor was incensed by this iniquitousness, and wrote a pamphlet defending Whitman as a wholesome patriot, greatly increasing his popularity. Further adding to Whitman's fame during this period was the publication of *O Captain! My Captain!*; a relatively conventional poem chronicling the death of Abraham Lincoln. It was the only poem to appear in anthologies during Whitman's lifetime. The author then moved onto work at the Attorney General's office, interviewing former Confederate soldiers for Presidential Pardons - an occupation which was more to Whitman's taste. He later wrote to a friend; 'there are real characters among them... and you know I have a fancy for anything out of the ordinary.' During this time, Whitman succeeded in finding a publisher for *Leaves of Grass* (eventually issued in 1871), the same year it was mistakenly reported that its author died in a railroad accident. Only two years after this great personal success, Whitman suffered a paralytic stroke (early in 1873) and was induced to move to the home of his brother in

New Jersey. Whilst there, he was very productive, publishing three versions of *Leaves of Grass*, as well as other works. This was also the last point at which Whitman was fully mobile, and he received many famous authors, including Oscar Wilde and Thomas Eakins. In 1884, he bought his own house, remaining in New Jersey, but became completely bedridden soon after. In the last week of his life, Whitman was too weak even to lift a knife or fork, and wrote; 'I suffer all the time: I have no relief, no escape: it is monotony—monotony—monotony—in pain.' He died from diminished lung capacity, the result of bronchial pneumonia and an abscess on the chest, on 26 March 1892.

By the time of his death, Whitman had become a veritable national celebrity, and a public viewing of his body was held at his home; an event which attracted over one thousand people in three hours. His coffin was barely visible because of all the flowers and wreaths. Whitman was buried four days later at Harleigh Cemetery in Camden, New Jersey. He has since been eulogised as America's first 'poet of democracy', due to his uncanny ability to write in the American character, and remains an enduring and much loved literary figure to this day.

PREFACE

Probably there are few who to-day question the propriety of publishing the love-letters of eminent persons a generation after the deaths of both parties to the correspondence. When one recalls the published love-letters of Abelard, of Dorothy Osborne, of Lady Hamilton, of Mary Wollstonecraft, of Margaret Fuller, of George Sand, Bismarck, Shelley, Victor Hugo, Edgar Allan Poe, and—to mention only one more illustrious example—of the Brownings, one must needs look upon this form of presenting biographical material as a well-established, if not a valuable, convention of letters.

As to the particular set of letters presented to the reader in this volume, a word of explanation and history may be required. Most of these letters are from Anne Gilchrist to Walt Whitman, a few are replies to her letters, and a few are letters from her children to Whitman. Mrs. Gilchrist died in 1885. When, two years later, her son, Herbert Harlakenden Gilchrist, was collecting material for his interesting biography of his mother, Whitman was asked for the letters that she had written to him—or rather for extracts from them. In reply to this request the poet said, "I do not know that I can furnish any good reason, but I feel to keep these utterances exclusively to myself. But I cannot let your book go to press without at least saying—and wishing it put on record— that among the perfect women I have met (and it has been my unspeakably good fortune to have had the very best, for mother, sisters, and friends) I have known none more perfect in every relation, than my dear, dear friend, Anne Gilchrist." But since Whitman carefully preserved them for twenty years, refusing to destroy them as he had destroyed such other written matter as he did not care to have preserved, it would appear that he intended that so beautiful a tribute to the poetry that he had written, no less than to the personality of the poet, should be included in that complete biography which is being slowly written, by many hands, of America's most unique man of genius. In any case, when these letters came into my hands in the apportionment of Whitman's literary legacy under the will which named me as one of his three literary executors, there were but three things which I could honourably do with them—rather, on closer analysis, there seemed to be but one. To leave them in *my* will or to place them in some public repository would have been to shift a responsibility which was evidently mine to the shoulders of others who, perhaps, would be in possession of fewer facts in the light of which to discharge that responsibility. To destroy them would be to do what Whitman should have done if it was to be done at all, and to erase forever one of the finest tributes that either the man or the poet ever received, one of the most touching self-revelations that a noble soul ever "poured out on paper." The remaining alternative was to edit and publish them (after keeping them a proper length of time), for the benefit, not only of the general reader, but as an aid to the future biographer who from the proper perspective will write the life of America's great poet and prophet. In this determination my judgment has been confirmed by that of the few sympathetic friends who, during the twenty-five years that the letters have been in my possession, have been allowed to read them.

It is a matter of regret that so few of Whitman's letters to Mrs. Gilchrist are available. Those included in this volume, sometimes in fragmentary form, have been taken from loose copies found among his papers after his death, or, in a few instances, are reprinted from Herbert Harlakenden Gilchrist's "Anne Gilchrist" or Horace Traubel's "With Walt Whitman in Camden." Acknowledgment of these latter is made in each instance. But though Whitman's letters printed in this correspondence will not compare with Mrs. Gilchrist's in point of number, enough are presented to suggest the tenor of them all.

As a matter of fact, the first love-letter from Anne Gilchrist to Walt Whitman was in the form of an essay written in his defense called "An Englishwoman's Estimate of Walt Whitman." For that reason this well-known essay is reprinted in this volume; and "A Confession of Faith," in reality an amplification of the "Estimate" written several years after the publication of the latter, is included. The reader who desires to follow the story of this friendship in a chronological order will do well to read at least the former of these tributes before beginning the letters. Indebtedness is acknowledged to Prof. Emory Halloway of Brooklyn, New York, for valuable suggestions.

T. B. H.

INTRODUCTION

Undoubtedly Mrs. Gilchrist's "Estimate of Walt Whitman," published in the (Boston) *Radical* in May, 1870, was the finest, as it was the first, public tribute ever paid to the poet by a woman. Whitman himself so considered it—"the proudest word that ever came to me from a woman—if not the proudest word of all from any source." But a finer tribute was to follow, in the sacred privacy of the love-letters which are now made public forty years and more after they were written. The purpose of this Introduction is not to interpret those letters, but to sketch the story in the light of which they are to be read. And since both Anne Gilchrist and Walt Whitman have had sympathetic and painstaking biographers, it will not be necessary here to mention at length the already known facts of their respective lives.

The story naturally begins with Whitman. He was born at West Hills, Long Island, New York, on May 31, 1819. His father was of English descent, and came of a family of sailors and farmers. His mother, to whom he himself attributed most of his personal qualities, was of excellent Hollandic stock. Moving to Brooklyn while still in frocks, he there passed his boyhood and youth, but took many summer trips to visit relatives in the country. He early left the public school for the printing offices of local newspapers, picking enough general knowledge to enable him, when about seventeen years of age, to teach schools in the rural districts of his native island. Very early in life he became a writer, chiefly of short prose tales and essays, which were accepted by the best New York magazines. His literary and journalistic work was not confined to the metropolis, but took him, for a few months in 1848, so far away from home as New Orleans. In 1851-54, besides writing for and editing newspapers, he was engaged in housebuilding, the trade of his father. Although this was, it is said, a profitable business, he gave it up to write poetry, and issued his first volume, "Leaves of Grass," in 1855. The book had been written with great pains, according to a preconceived plan of the author to be stated in the preface; and it was finally set up (by his own hands, for want of a publisher) only, as he tells us, after many "doings and undoings, leaving out the stock 'poetical' touches." Its publication was the occasion of probably the most voluminous controversy of American letters—mostly abuse, ridicule, and condemnation.

In 1862 Whitman's brother George, who had volunteered in the Union Army, was reported badly wounded in the Fredericksburg fight. Walt, going at once to the war front in Virginia, found that his brother's wound was not serious enough to require his ministrations, but gradually he became engaged in nursing other wounded soldiers, until this work, as a volunteer hospital missionary in Washington, engrossed the major part of his time. This continued until and for some years after the end of the war. Whitman's own needs were supplied by occasional literary work and from his earnings as a clerk first in the Interior and later in the Attorney General's Department. He had gone to Washington a man of strong and majestic physique, but his untiring devotion, fidelity, and vigilance in nursing the sick and wounded soldiers in the army hospitals in and about Washington was soon to shatter that constitution which was ever a marvel to its possessor, and to condemn him to pass the last two decades of his life in unaccustomed invalidism. The history of the Civil War in America presents no instance of nobler fulfilment of duty or of sublimer sacrifice.

Meanwhile his muse was not neglected. His book had gone through four editions, and, with the increment of the noble war poetry of "Drum Taps," had become a volume of size. At a very early period "Leaves of Grass" had been hailed as an important literary contribution by a few of the best thinkers in this country and in England but, generally speaking, nearly all literary persons received it with much criticism and many qualifications. In

Washington devoted disciples like William Douglas O'Connor and John Burroughs never varied in their uncompromising adherence to the book and its author. This appreciation only by the few was likewise encountered in England. The book had made a stir among the literary classes, but its importance was not at all generally recognized. Men like John Addington Symonds, Edward Dowden, and William Michael Rossetti were, however, almost unrestricted in their praise.

It was William Rossetti who planned, in 1867, to bring out in England a volume of selections from Whitman's poetry, in the belief that it was better to leave out the poems that had provoked such adverse criticism, in order to get Whitman a foothold among those who might prefer to have an expurgated edition. Whitman's attitude toward the plan at the time is given in a letter which he wrote to Rossetti on December 3, 1867: "I cannot and will not consent of my own volition to countenance an expurgated edition of my pieces. I have steadily refused to do so under seductive offers, here in my own country, and must not do so in another country." It appeared, however, that Rossetti had already advanced his project, and Whitman graciously added: "If, before the arrival of this letter, you have practically invested in, and accomplished, or partially accomplished, any plan, even contrary to this letter, I do not expect you to abandon it, at loss of outlay; but shall *bona fide* consider you blameless if you let it go on, and be carried out, as you may have arranged. It is the question of the authorization of an expurgated edition proceeding from me, that deepest engages me. The facts of the different ways, one way or another way, in which the book may appear in England, out of influences not under the shelter of my umbrage, are of much less importance to me. After making the foregoing explanation, I shall, I think, accept kindly whatever happens. For I feel, indeed know, that I am in the hands of a friend, and that my pieces will receive that truest, brightest of light and perception coming from love. In that, all other and lesser requisites become pale...." The Rossetti "Selections" duly appeared—with what momentous influence upon the two persons whose friendship we are tracing will presently be shown.

On June 22, 1869, Anne Gilchrist, writing to Rossetti, said: "I was calling on Madox Brown a fortnight ago, and he put into my hands your edition of Walt Whitman's poems. I shall not cease to thank him for that. Since I have had it, I can read no other book: it holds me entirely spellbound, and I go through it again and again with deepening delight and wonder. How can one refrain from expressing gratitude to you for what you have so admirably done?..." To this Rossetti promptly responded: "Your letter has given me keen pleasure this morning. That glorious man Whitman will one day be known as one of the greatest sons of Earth, a few steps below Shakespeare on the throne of immortality. What a tearing-away of the obscuring veil of use and wont from the visage of man and of life! I am doing myself the pleasure of at once ordering a copy of the "Selections" for you, which you will be so kind as to accept. Genuine—i. e., *enthusiastic*—appreciators are not so common, and must be cultivated when they appear.... Anybody who values Whitman as you do ought to read the whole of him...." At a later date Rossetti gave Mrs. Gilchrist a copy of the complete "Leaves of Grass," in acknowledging which she said, "The gift of yours I have not any words to tell you how priceless it will be to me...." This lengthy letter was later, at Rossetti's solicitation, worked over for publication as the "Estimate of Walt Whitman" to which reference has already been made.

Anne Gilchrist was primarily a woman of letters. Though her natural bent was toward science and philosophy, her marriage threw her into association with artists and writers of *belles lettres*. She was born in London on February 25, 1828. She came of excellent ancestry, and received a good education, particularly in music. She had a profoundly religious nature, although it appears that she was never a believer in many of the orthodox Christian doctrines. Very early in life she recognized the greatness of such men as Emerson and Comte. In 1851, at the age of twenty-three, she married Alexander Gilchrist, two months her junior. Though of limited means, he possessed literary ability and was then preparing for the bar. His early writings secured for him the friendship of Carlyle, who for years lived next door to the Gilchrists in Cheyne Row. This friendship led to others, and the Gilchrists were soon introduced into that supreme literary circle which included Ruskin, Herbert Spencer, George Eliot, the Rossettis, Tennyson, and many another great mind of that illustrious age.

Within ten years of their marriage the Gilchrists had four children, in whom they were very happy. But in the year 1861, when Anne was thirty-three years of age, her husband died. It was a terrible blow, but she faced the future unflinchingly, and reared her children, giving to each of them a profession. At the time of her husband's death his life of William Blake was nearing completion. With the assistance of William and Gabriel Rossetti Mrs. Gilchrist finished the work on this excellent biography, and it was published by Macmillan. Whitman has paid a fitting tribute to the pluck exhibited in this achievement: "Do you know much of Blake?" said Whitman to Horace Traubel, who records the conversation in his remarkable book "With Walt Whitman in Camden." "You know, this is Mrs. Gilchrist's book—the book she completed. They had made up their minds to do the work—her husband had it well under way: he caught a fever and was carried off. Mrs. Gilchrist was left with four young children, alone: her perplexities were great. Have you noticed that the time to look for the best things in best people is the moment of their greatest need? Look at Lincoln: he is our proudest example: he proved to be big as, bigger than, any emergency—his grasp was a giant's grasp—made dark things light, made hard things easy.... (Mrs. Gilchrist) belonged to the same noble breed: seized the reins, was competent; her head was clear, her hand was firm."

The circumstances under which she first read Whitman's poetry have been narrated. When in 1869 Whitman became aware of the Rossetti correspondence, he felt greatly honoured, and through Rossetti he sent his portrait to the as yet anonymous lady. In acknowledging this communication his English friend has a grateful word from "the lady" to return: "I gave your letter, and the second copy of your portrait, to the lady you refer to, and need scarcely say how truly delighted she was. She has asked me to say that you could not have devised for her a more welcome pleasure, and that she feels grateful to me for having sent to America the extracts from what she had written, since they have been a satisfaction to you...." Early in 1870 the "Estimate" appeared in the *Radical*, still more than a year before Mrs. Gilchrist addressed her first letter to Whitman. He welcomed the essay, and its author as a new and peculiarly powerful champion of "Leaves of Grass." To Rossetti he wrote: "I am deeply touched by these sympathies and convictions, coming from a woman and from England, and am sure that if the lady knew how much comfort it has been to me to get them, she would not only pardon you for transmitting them but approve that action. I realize indeed of this smiling and emphatic *well done* from the heart and conscience of a true wife and mother, and one, too, whose sense of the poetic, as I glean from your letter, after flowing through the heart and conscience, must also move through and satisfy science as much as the esthetic, that I had hitherto received no eulogium so magnificent." Concerning this experience Whitman said to Horace Traubel, at a much later period: "You can imagine what such a thing as her 'Estimate' meant to me at that time. Almost everybody was against me—the papers, the preachers, the literary gentlemen—nearly everybody with only here and there a dissenting voice—when it looked on the surface as if my enterprise was bound to fail ... then this wonderful woman. Such things stagger a man ... I had got so used to being ignored or denounced that the appearance of a friend was always accompanied with a sort of shock.... There are shocks that knock you up, shocks that knock you down. Mrs. Gilchrist never wavered from her first decision. I have that sort of feeling about her which cannot easily be spoken of—...: love (strong personal love, too), reverence, respect—you see, it won't go into words: all the words are weak and formal." Speaking again of her first criticism of his work, he said: "I remember well how one of my noblest, best friends—one of my wisest, cutest, profoundest, most candid critics—how Mrs. Gilchrist, even to the last, insisted that "Leaves of Grass" was not the mouthpiece of parlours, refinements—no—but the language of strength, power, passion, intensity, absorption, sincerity...." He claimed a closer relationship to her than he allowed to Rossetti: "Rossetti mentions Mrs. Gilchrist. Well, he had a right to—almost as much right as I had: a sort of brother's right: she was his friend, she was more than my friend. I feel like Hamlet when he said forty thousand brothers could not feel what he felt for Ophelia. After all ... we were a family—a happy family: the few of us who got together, going with love the same way—we were a happy family. The crowd was on the other side but we were on our side—we: a few of us, just a few: and despite our paucity of numbers we made ourselves tell for the good cause."

From these expressions it is quite clear that Whitman's attitude toward Mrs. Gilchrist was at first that of the unpopular prophet who finds a worthy and welcome disciple in an unexpected place. And that he should have so felt was but natural, for she had been drawn to him, as she confided to him in one of her letters, by what he had written rather than and not by her knowledge of the man. There can be no doubt, however, that on Mrs. Gilchrist's part something more than the friendship of her new-found liberator was desired. When she read the "Leaves of Grass" she was forty-one years of age, in the full vigour of womanhood. To her the reading meant a new birth, causing her to pour out her soul to the prophet and poet across the seas with a freedom and abandon that were phenomenal. This was in the first letter printed in this volume, under date of September 3, 1871, and about the time that Whitman had sent to his new supporter a copy of his poems. Perhaps the strongest reason why Whitman did not reply to passion with passion lies in the fact that his heart was, so far as attachments of that sort were concerned, already bestowed elsewhere. I am indebted to Professor Holloway for the information that Whitman was, in 1864, the unfortunate lover of a certain lady whose previous marriage to another, while it did not dim their mutual devotion, did serve to keep them apart. To her Whitman wrote that heart-wrung lyric of separation, "Out of the rolling ocean, the crowd." This suggests that there was probably a double tragedy, so ironical is the fate of the affections, Anne Gilchrist and Walt Whitman both passionately yearning for personal love yet unable to quench the one desire in the other.

But if there could not be between them the love which leads to marriage, there could be a noble and tender and life-long friendship. Over this Whitman's loss of his magnificent health, to be followed by an invalidism of twenty years, had no power. In 1873 Whitman was stricken with paralysis, which rendered him so helpless that he had to give up his work and finally his position, and to go to live for the rest of his life in Camden, New Jersey. Mrs. Gilchrist's affection for him did not waver when this trial was made of it. Indeed, his illness had the effect, as these letters show, of quickening the desire which she had had for several years (since 1869) of coming to live in America, that she might be near him to lighten his burdens, and, if she could not hope to cherish him as a wife, that she might at least care for him as a mother. Whitman, it will be noted, strongly advised against this plan. Just why he wished to keep her away from America is unclear, possibly because he dared not put so idealistic a friendship and discipleship to the test of personal acquaintance with a prematurely broken old man. Nevertheless, on August 30, 1876, Mrs. Gilchrist set sail, with three of her children, for Philadelphia. They arrived in September. From that date until the spring of 1878 the Gilchrists kept house at 1929 North Twenty-second street, Philadelphia, where Whitman was a frequent and regular visitor.

It is interesting to note that Mrs. Gilchrist's appreciation of Whitman did not lessen after she had met and known him in the intimacy of that tea-table circle which at her house discussed the same great variety of topics—literature, religion, science, politics—that had enlivened the O'Connor breakfast table in Washington. She shall describe it and him herself. In a letter to Rossetti, under date of December 22, 1876, she writes: "But I need not tell you that our greatest pleasure is the society of Mr. Whitman, who fully realizes the ideal I had formed from his poems, and brings such an atmosphere of cordiality and geniality with him as is indescribable. He is really making slow but, I trust, steady progress toward recovery, having been much cheered (and no doubt that acted favourably upon his health) by the sympathy manifested toward him in England and the pleasure of finding so many buyers of his poems there. It must be a deep satisfaction to you to have been the channel through which this help and comfort flowed...." And a year later she writes to the same correspondent: "We are having delightful evenings this winter; how often do I wish you could make one in the circle around our tea table where sits on my right hand every evening but Sunday Walt Whitman. He has made great progress in health and recovered powers of getting about during the year we have been here: nevertheless the lameness—the dragging instead of lifting the left leg continues; and this together with his white hair and beard give him a look of age curiously contradicted by his face, which has not only the ruddy freshness but the full, rounded contours of youth, nowhere drawn or wrinkled or sunk; it is a face as indicative of serenity and goodness and of mental and bodily health as the brow is of intellectual power. But I notice he occasionally speaks of himself as having a 'wounded brain,' and of being still quite altered from his former self."

Whitman, on his part, thoroughly enjoyed the afternoon sunshine of such friendly hospitality, for he considered Mrs. Gilchrist even more gifted as a conversationalist than as a writer. For hints of the sort of talk that flowed with Mrs. Gilchrist's tea I must refer the reader to her son's realistic biography.

After two years of residence in Philadelphia, the Gilchrists went to dwell in Boston and later in New York City, and met the leaders in the two literary capitals. From these addresses the letters begin again, after the natural interruption of two years. It is at this time that the first letters from Herbert and Beatrice Gilchrist were written. These are given in this volume to complete the chain and to show how completely they were in sympathy with their mother in their love and appreciation of Whitman. From New York they all sailed for their old home in England on June 7, 1879. Whitman came the day before to wish them good voyage. The chief reason for the return to England seems to have been the desire to send Beatrice to Berne to complete her medical education. After the return to England, or rather while they are still en route at Glasgow, the letters begin again.

Several years of literary work yet remained to Mrs. Gilchrist. The chief writings of these years were a new edition of the Blake, a life of Mary Lamb for the Eminent Women Series, an article on Blake for the Dictionary of National Biography, several essays including "Three Glimpses of a New England Village," and the "Confession of Faith." She was beginning a careful study of the life and writings of Carlyle, with the intention of writing a life of her old friend to reply to the aspersions of Freude. This last work was, however, never completed, for early in 1882 some malady which rendered her breathing difficult had already begun to cast the shadow of death upon her. But her faith, long schooled in the optimism of "Leaves of Grass," looked upon the steadily approaching end with calmness. On November 29, 1885, she died.

When Whitman was informed of her death by Herbert Gilchrist, he could find words for only the following brief reply:

15th December 1885.
Camden, United States, America.

Dear Herbert:

I have received your letter. Nothing now remains but a

sweet and rich memory—none more beautiful all time, all life all the earth—I cannot write anything of a letter to-day. I must sit alone and think.

Walt Whitman.

Later, in conversations with Horace Traubel which the latter has preserved in his minute biography of Whitman, he was able to express his regard for Mrs. Gilchrist more fully—"a supreme character of whom the world knows too little for its own good ... If her sayings had been recorded—I do not say she would pale, but I do say she would equal the best of the women of our century— add something as great as any to the testimony on the side of her sex." And at another time: "Oh! she was strangely different from the average; entirely herself; as simple as nature; true, honest; beautiful as a tree is tall, leafy, rich, full, free—*is* a tree. Yet, free as she was by nature, bound by no conventionalisms, she was the most courageous of women; more than queenly; of high aspect in the best sense. She was not cold; she had her passions; I have known her to warm up—to resent something that was said; some impeachment of good things—great things; of a person sometimes; she had the largest charity, the sweetest fondest optimism.... She was a radical of radicals; enjoyed all sorts of high enthusiasms: was exquisitely sensitized; belonged to the times yet to come; her vision went on and on."

This searching interpretation of her character wants only her artist son's description of her personal appearance to make the final picture complete: "A little above the average height, she walked with an even, light step. Brown hair concealed a full and finely chiselled brow, and her hazel eyes bent upon you a bright and penetrating gaze. Whilst conversing her face became radiant as with an experience of golden years; humour was present in her conversation—flecks of sunshine, such as sometimes play about the minds of deeply religious natures. Her animated manner seldom flagged, and charmed the taciturn to talking in his or her best humour." Once, when speaking to Walt Whitman of the beauty of the human speaking voice, he replied: "The voice indicates the soul. Hers, with its varied modulations and blended tones, was the tenderest, most musical voice ever to bless our ears."

Her death was a long-lasting shock to Whitman. "She was a wonderful woman—a sort of human miracle to me.... Her taking off ... was a great shock to me: I have never quite got over it: she was near to me: she was subtle: her grasp on my work was tremendous—so sure, so all around, so adequate." If this sounds a trifle self-centred in its criticism, not so was the poem which, in memory of her, he wrote as a fitting epitaph from the poet she had loved.

"GOING SOMEWHERE"

My science-friend, my noblest woman-friend (Now buried
    in an English grave—and this a memory-leaf for her
    dear sake),
Ended our talk—"The sum, concluding all we know of old
    or modern learning, intuitions deep,
Of all Geologies—Histories—of all Astronomy—of
    Evolution, Metaphysics all,
Is, that we all are onward, onward, speeding slowly, surely
    bettering,
Life, life an endless march, an endless army (no halt, but, it
    is duly over),
The world, the race, the soul—in space and time the
    universes,
All bound as is befitting each—all surely going somewhere."

A WOMAN'S
ESTIMATE OF WALT WHITMAN[1]

FROM LETTERS BY
ANNE GILCHRIST TO W. M. ROSSETTI.

June 23, 1869.—I am very sure you are right in your estimate of Walt Whitman. There is nothing in him that I shall ever let go my hold of. For me the reading of his poems is truly a new birth of the soul.

I shall quite fearlessly accept your kind offer of the loan of a complete edition, certain that great and divinely beautiful nature has not, could not infuse any poison into the wine he has poured out for us. And as for what you specially allude to, who so well able to bear it—I will say, to judge wisely of it—as one who, having been a happy wife and mother, has learned to accept all things with tenderness, to feel a sacredness in all? Perhaps Walt Whitman has forgotten—or, through some theory in his head, has overridden—the truth that our instincts are beautiful facts of nature, as well as our bodies; and that we have a strong instinct of silence about some things.

July 11.—I think it was very manly and kind of you to put the whole of Walt Whitman's poems into my hands; and that I have no other friend who would have judged them and me so wisely and generously.

I had not dreamed that words could cease to be words, and become electric streams like these. I do assure you that, strong as I am, I feel sometimes as if I had not bodily strength to read many of these poems. In the series headed "Calamus," for instance, in some of the "Songs of Parting," the "Voice out of the Sea," the poem beginning "Tears, Tears," &c., there is such a weight of emotion, such a tension of the heart, that mine refuses to beat under it,—stands quite still,—and I am obliged to lay the book down for a while. Or again, in the piece called "Walt Whitman," and one or two others of that type, I am as one hurried through stormy seas, over high mountains, dazed with sunlight, stunned with a crowd and tumult of faces and voices, till I am breathless, bewildered, half dead. Then come parts and whole poems in which there is such calm wisdom and strength of thought, such a cheerful breadth of sunshine, that the soul bathes in them renewed and strengthened. Living impulses flow out of these that make me exult in life, yet look longingly towards "the superb vistas of Death." Those who admire this poem, and don't care for that, and talk of formlessness, absence of metre, &c., are quite as far from any genuine recognition of Walt Whitman as his bitter detractors. Not, of course, that all the pieces are equal in power and beauty, but that all are vital; they grew—they were not made. We criticise a palace or a cathedral; but what is the good of criticising a forest? Are not the hitherto-accepted masterpieces of literature akin rather to noble architecture; built up of material rendered precious by elaboration; planned with subtile art that makes beauty go hand in hand with rule and measure, and knows where the last stone will come, before the first is laid; the result stately, fixed, yet such as might, in every particular, have been different from what it is (therefore inviting criticism), contrasting proudly with the careless freedom of nature, opposing its own rigid adherence to symmetry to her willful dallying with it? But not such is this book. Seeds brought by the winds from north, south, east, and west, lying long in the earth, not resting on it like the stately building, but hid in and assimilating it, shooting upwards to be nourished by the air and the sunshine and the rain which beat idly against that,—each bough and twig and leaf growing in strength and beauty its own way, a law to itself, yet, with all this freedom of spontaneous growth, the result inevitable, unalterable (therefore setting criticism at naught), above all things, vital,—that is, a source of ever-generating vitality: such are these poems.

> "Roots and leaves themselves alone are these,
> Scents brought to men and women from the wild woods
>   and from the pondside,
> Breast sorrel and pinks of love, fingers that wind around
>   tighter than vines,
> Gushes from the throats of birds hid in the foliage of trees
>   as the sun is risen,
> Breezes of land and love, breezes set from living shores out
>   to you on the living sea,—to you, O sailors!
> Frost-mellowed berries and Third-month twigs, offered
>   fresh to young persons wandering out in the fields when
>   the winter breaks up,
> Love-buds put before you and within you, whoever you are,
> Buds to be unfolded on the old terms.
> If you bring the warmth of the sun to them, they will open,
>   and bring form, colour, perfume, to you:
> If you become the aliment and the wet, they will become
>   flowers, fruits, tall branches and trees."

And the music takes good care of itself, too. As if it *could* be otherwise! As if those "large, melodious thoughts," those emotions, now so stormy and wild, now of unfathomed tenderness and gentleness, could fail to vibrate through the words in strong, sweeping, long-sustained chords, with lovely melodies winding in and out fitfully amongst them! Listen, for instance, to the penetrating sweetness, set in the midst of rugged grandeur, of the passage beginning,—

> "I am he that walks with the tender and growing night;
> I call to the earth and sea half held by the night."

I see that no counting of syllables will reveal the mechanism of the music; and that this rushing spontaneity could not stay to bind itself with the fetters of metre. But I know that the music

31

is there, and that I would not for something change ears with those who cannot hear it. And I know that poetry must do one of two things,—either own this man as equal with her highest completest manifestors, or stand aside, and admit that there is something come into the world nobler, diviner than herself, one that is free of the universe, and can tell its secrets as none before.

I do not think or believe this; but see it with the same unmistakable definiteness of perception and full consciousness that I see the sun at this moment in the noonday sky, and feel his rays glowing down upon me as I write in the open air. What more can you ask of the works of a man's mouth than that they should "absorb into you as food and air, to appear again in your strength, gait, face,"—that they should be "fibre and filter to your blood," joy and gladness to your whole nature?

I am persuaded that one great source of this kindling, vitalizing power—I suppose *the* great source—is the grasp laid upon the present, the fearless and comprehensive dealing with reality. Hitherto the leaders of thought have (except in science) been men with their faces resolutely turned backwards; men who have made of the past a tyrant that beggars and scorns the present, hardly seeing any greatness but what is shrouded away in the twilight, underground past; naming the present only for disparaging comparisons, humiliating distrust that tends to create the very barrenness it complains of; bidding me warm myself at fires that went out to mortal eyes centuries ago; insisting, in religion above all, that I must either "look through dead men's eyes," or shut my own in helpless darkness. Poets fancying themselves so happy over the chill and faded beauty of the past, but not making me happy at all,—rebellious always at being dragged down out of the free air and sunshine of to-day.

But this poet, this "athlete, full of rich words, full of joy," takes you by the hand, and turns you with your face straight forwards. The present is great enough for him, because he is great enough for it. It flows through him as a "vast oceanic tide," lifting up a mighty voice. Earth, "the eloquent, dumb, great mother," is not old, has lost none of her fresh charms, none of her divine meanings; still bears great sons and daughters, if only they would possess themselves and accept their birthright,—a richer, not a poorer, heritage than was ever provided before,—richer by all the toil and suffering of the generations that have preceded, and by the further unfolding of the eternal purposes. Here is one come at last who can show them how; whose songs are the breath of a glad, strong, beautiful life, nourished sufficingly, kindled to unsurpassed intensity and greatness by the gifts of the present.

"Each moment and whatever happens thrills me with joy."

"O the joy of my soul leaning poised on itself,—receiving
    identity through materials, and loving them,—
    observing characters, and absorbing them!
O my soul vibrated back to me from them!

"O the gleesome saunter over fields and hillsides!
The leaves and flowers of the commonest weeds, the moist,
    fresh stillness of the woods,
The exquisite smell of the earth at daybreak, and all through
    the forenoon.

"O to realize space!
The plenteousness of all—that there are no bounds;
To emerge, and be of the sky—of the sun and moon and the
    flying clouds, as one with them.

"O the joy of suffering,—
To struggle against great odds, to meet enemies undaunted,
To be entirely alone with them—to find how much one can
    stand!"

I used to think it was great to disregard happiness, to press on to a high goal, careless, disdainful of it. But now I see that there is nothing so great as to be capable of happiness; to pluck it out of "each moment and whatever happens"; to find that one can ride as gay and buoyant on the angry, menacing, tumultuous waves of life as on those that glide and glitter under a clear sky; that it is not defeat and wretchedness which come out of the storm of adversity, but strength and calmness.

See, again, in the pieces gathered together under the title "Calamus," and elsewhere, what it means for a man to love his fellow-man. Did you dream it before? These "evangel-poems of comrades and of love" speak, with the abiding, penetrating power of prophecy, of a "new and superb friendship"; speak not as beautiful dreams, unrealizable aspirations to be laid aside in sober moods, because they breathe out what now glows within the poet's own breast, and flows out in action toward the men around him. Had ever any land before her poet, not only to concentrate within himself her life, and, when she kindled with anger against her children who were treacherous to the cause her life is bound up with, to announce and justify her terrible purpose in words of unsurpassable grandeur (as in the poem beginning, "Rise, O days, from your fathomless deeps"), but also to go and with his own hands dress the wounds, with his powerful presence soothe and sustain and nourish her suffering soldiers,—hundreds of them, thousands, tens of thousands,—by day and by night, for weeks, months, years?

> "I sit by the restless all the dark night; some are so young,
> Some suffer so much: I recall the experience sweet and sad.
> Many a soldier's loving arms about this neck have crossed
>   and rested,
> Many a soldier's kiss dwells on these bearded lips:—"

Kisses, that touched with the fire of a strange, new, undying eloquence the lips that received them! The most transcendent genius could not, untaught by that "experience sweet and sad," have breathed out hymns for her dead soldiers of such ineffably tender, sorrowful, yet triumphant beauty.

But the present spreads before us other things besides those of which it is easy to see the greatness and beauty; and the poet would leave us to learn the hardest part of our lesson unhelped if he took no heed of these; and would be unfaithful to his calling, as interpreter of man to himself and of the scheme of things in relation to him, if he did not accept all—if he did not teach "the great lesson of reception, neither preference nor denial." If he feared to stretch out the hand, not of condescending pity, but of fellowship, to the degraded, criminal, foolish, despised, knowing that they are only laggards in "the great procession winding along the roads of the universe," "the far-behind to come on in their turn," knowing the "amplitude of Time," how could he roll the stone of contempt off the heart as he does, and cut the strangling knot of the problem of inherited viciousness and degradation? And, if he were not bold and true to the utmost, and did not own in himself the threads of darkness mixed in with the threads of light, and own it with the same strength and directness that he tells of the light, and not in those vague generalities that everybody uses, and nobody means, in speaking on this head,—in the worst, germs of all that is in the best; in the best, germs of all that is in the worst,—the *brotherhood* of the human race would be a mere flourish of rhetoric. And brotherhood is naught if it does not bring brother's love along with it. If the poet's heart were not "a measureless ocean of love" that seeks the lips and would quench the thirst of all, he were not the one we have waited for so long. Who but he could put at last the right meaning into that word "democracy," which has been made to bear such a burthen of incongruous notions?

> "By God! I will have nothing that all cannot have their
> counterpart of on the same terms!"

flashing it forth like a banner, making it draw the instant allegiance of every man and woman who loves justice. All occupations, however homely, all developments of the activities of man, need the poet's recognition, because every man needs the assurance that for him also the materials out of which to build up a great and satisfying life lie to hand, the sole magic in the use of them, all of the right stuff in the right hands. Hence those patient enumerations of every conceivable kind of industry:—

> "In them far more than you estimated—in them far less
> also."

Far more as a means, next to nothing as an end: whereas we are wont to take it the other way, and think the result something, but the means a weariness. Out of all come strength, and the cheerfulness of strength. I murmured not a little, to say the truth, under these enumerations, at first. But now I think that not only is their purpose a justification, but that the musical ear and vividness of perception of the poet have enabled him to perform this task also with strength and grace, and that they are harmonious as well as necessary parts of the great whole.

Nor do I sympathize with those who grumble at the unexpected words that turn up now and then. A quarrel with words is always, more or less, a quarrel with meanings; and here we are to be as genial and as wide as nature, and quarrel with nothing. If the thing a word stands for exists by divine appointment (and what does not so exist?), the word need never be ashamed of itself; the shorter and more direct, the better. It is a gain to make friends with it, and see it in good company. Here at all events, "poetic diction" would not serve,—not pretty, soft, colourless words, laid by in lavender for the special uses of poetry, that have had none of the wear and tear of daily life; but such as have stood most, as tell of human heart-beats, as fit closest to the sense, and have taken deep hues of association from the varied experiences of life—those are the words wanted here. We only ask to seize and be seized swiftly, over-masteringly, by the great meanings. We see with the eyes of the soul, listen with the ears of the soul; the poor old words that have served so many generations for purposes, good, bad, and indifferent, and become warped and blurred in the process, grow young again, regenerate, translucent. It is not mere delight they give us,—*that* the "sweet singers," with their subtly wrought gifts, their mellifluous speech, can give too in their degree; it is such life and health as enable us to pluck delights for ourselves out of every hour of the day, and taste the sunshine that ripened the corn in the crust we eat (I often seem to myself to do that).

Out of the scorn of the present came skepticism; and out of the large, loving acceptance of it comes faith. If *now* is so great and beautiful, I need no arguments to make me believe that the *nows* of the past and of the future were and will be great and beautiful, too.

"I know I am deathless.
I know this orbit of mine cannot be swept by the carpenter's
    compass.
I know I shall not pass, like a child's carlacue cut with a
    burnt stick at night.
I know I am august.
I do not trouble my spirit to vindicate itself or be
    understood.

"My foothold is tenoned and mortised in granite:
I laugh at what you call dissolution,
And I know the amplitude of Time."

"No array of terms can say how much I am at peace about
    God and Death."

You argued rightly that my confidence would not be betrayed by any of the poems in this book. None of them troubled me even for a moment; because I saw at a glance that it was not, as men had supposed, the heights brought down to the depths, but the depths lifted up level with the sunlit heights, that they might become clear and sunlit, too. Always, for a woman, a veil woven out of her own soul—never touched upon even, with a rough hand, by this poet. But, for a man, a daring, fearless pride in himself, not a mock-modesty woven out of delusions—a very poor imitation of a woman's. Do they not see that this fearless pride, this complete acceptance of themselves, is needful for her pride, her justification? What! is it all so ignoble, so base, that it will not bear the honest light of speech from lips so gifted with "the divine power to use words?" Then what hateful, bitter humiliation for her, to have to give herself up to the reality! Do you think there is ever a bride who does not taste more or less this bitterness in her cup? But who put it there? It must surely be man's fault, not God's, that she has to say to herself, "Soul, look another way—you have no part in this. Motherhood is beautiful, fatherhood is beautiful; but the dawn of fatherhood and motherhood is not beautiful." Do they really think that God is ashamed of what he has made and appointed? And, if not, surely it is somewhat superfluous that they should undertake to be so for him.

> "The full-spread pride of man is calming and excellent to
> the soul,"

Of a woman above all. It is true that instinct of silence I spoke of is a beautiful, imperishable part of nature, too. But it is not beautiful when it means an ignominious shame brooding darkly. Shame is like a very flexible veil, that follows faithfully the shape of what it covers,—beautiful when it hides a beautiful thing, ugly when it hides an ugly one. It has not covered what was beautiful here; it has covered a mean distrust of a man's self and of his Creator. It was needed that this silence, this evil spell, should for once be broken, and the daylight let in, that the dark cloud lying under might be scattered to the winds. It was needed that one who could here indicate for us "the path between reality and the soul" should speak. That is what these beautiful, despised poems, the "Children of Adam," do, read by the light that glows out of the rest of the volume: light of a clear, strong faith in God, of an unfathomably deep and tender love for humanity,—light shed out of a soul that is "possessed of itself."

"Natural life of me faithfully praising things,
Corroborating for ever the triumph of things."

Now silence may brood again; but lovingly, happily, as protecting what is beautiful, not as hiding what is unbeautiful; consciously enfolding a sweet and sacred mystery—august even as the mystery of Death, the dawn as the setting: kindred grandeurs, which to eyes that are opened shed a hallowing beauty on all that surrounds and preludes them.

"O vast and well-veiled Death!

"O the beautiful touch of Death, soothing and benumbing a
few moments, for reasons!"

He who can thus look with fearlessness at the beauty of Death may well dare to teach us to look with fearless, untroubled eyes at the perfect beauty of Love in all its appointed realizations. Now none need turn away their thoughts with pain or shame; though only lovers and poets may say what they will,—the lover to his own, the poet to all, because all are in a sense his own. None need fear that this will be harmful to the woman. How should there be such a flaw in the scheme of creation that, for the two with whom there is no complete life, save in closest sympathy, perfect union, what is natural and happy for the one should be baneful to the other? The utmost faithful freedom of speech, such as there is in these poems, creates in her no thought or feeling that shuns the light of heaven, none that are not as innocent and serenely fair as the flowers that grow; would lead, not to harm, but to such deep and tender affection as makes harm or the thought of harm simply impossible. Far more beautiful care than man is aware of has been taken in the making of her, to fit her to be his mate. God has taken such care that *he* need take none; none, that is, which consists in disguisement, insincerity, painful hushing-up of his true, grand, initiating nature. And, as regards the poet's utterances, which, it might be thought, however harmless in themselves, would prove harmful by falling into the hands of those for whom they are manifestly unsuitable, I believe that even here fear is needless. For her innocence is folded round with such thick folds of ignorance, till the right way and time for it to accept knowledge, that what is unsuitable is also unintelligible to her; and, if no dark shadow from without be cast on the white page by misconstruction or by foolish mystery and hiding away of it, no hurt will ensue from its passing freely through her hands.

This is so, though it is little understood or realized by men. Wives and mothers will learn through the poet that there is rejoicing grandeur and beauty there wherein their hearts have so longed to find it; where foolish men, traitors to themselves, poorly comprehending the grandeur of their own or the beauty of a woman's nature, have taken such pains to make her believe there was none,—nothing but miserable discrepancy.

One of the hardest things to make a child understand is, that down underneath your feet, if you go far enough, you come to blue sky and stars again; that there really is no "down" for the world, but only in every direction an "up." And that this is an all-embracing truth, including within its scope every created thing, and, with deepest significance, every part, faculty, attribute, healthful impulse, mind, and body of a man (each and all facing towards and related to the Infinite on every side), is what we grown children find it hardest to realize, too. Novalis said, "We touch heaven when we lay our hand on the human body"; which, if it mean anything, must mean an ample justification of the poet who has dared to be the poet of the body as well as of the soul,— to treat it with the freedom and grandeur of an ancient sculptor.

"Not physiognomy alone nor brain alone is worthy of the
    muse:—I say the form complete is worthier far.
"These are not parts and poems of the body only, but of the
    soul.
"O, I say now these are soul."

But while Novalis—who gazed at the truth a long way off,
up in the air, in a safe, comfortable, German fashion—has been
admiringly quoted by high authorities, the great American who
has dared to rise up and wrestle with it, and bring it alive and full
of power in the midst of us, has been greeted with a very different
kind of reception, as has happened a few times before in the
world in similar cases. Yet I feel deeply persuaded that a perfectly
fearless, candid, ennobling treatment of the life of the body (so
inextricably intertwined with, so potent in its influence on the
life of the soul) will prove of inestimable value to all earnest and
aspiring natures, impatient of the folly of the long-prevalent
belief that it is because of the greatness of the spirit that it has
learned to despise the body, and to ignore its influences; knowing
well that it is, on the contrary, just because the spirit is not great
enough, not healthy and vigorous enough, to transfuse itself into
the life of the body, elevating that and making it holy by its own
triumphant intensity; knowing, too, how the body avenges this
by dragging the soul down to the level assigned itself. Whereas
the spirit must lovingly embrace the body, as the roots of a tree
embrace the ground, drawing thence rich nourishment, warmth,
impulse. Or, rather, the body is itself the root of the soul—that
whereby it grows and feeds. The great tide of healthful life that
carries all before it must surge through the whole man, not beat
to and fro in one corner of his brain.

"O the life of my senses and flesh, transcending my senses
    and flesh!"

For the sake of all that is highest, a truthful recognition of this life, and especially of that of it which underlies the fundamental ties of humanity—the love of husband and wife, fatherhood, motherhood—is needed. Religion needs it, now at last alive to the fact that the basis of all true worship is comprised in "the great lesson of reception, neither preference nor denial," interpreting, loving, rejoicing in all that is created, fearing and despising nothing.

"I accept reality, and dare not question it."

The dignity of a man, the pride and affection of a woman, need it too. And so does the intellect. For science has opened up such elevating views of the mystery of material existence that, if poetry had not bestirred herself to handle this theme in her own way, she would have been left behind by her plodding sister. Science knows that matter is not, as we fancied, certain stolid atoms which the forces of nature vibrate through and push and pull about; but that the forces and the atoms are one mysterious, imperishable identity, neither conceivable without the other. She knows, as well as the poet, that destructibility is not one of nature's words; that it is only the relationship of things— tangibility, visibility—that are transitory. She knows that body and soul are one, and proclaims it undauntedly, regardless, and rightly regardless, of inferences. Timid onlookers, aghast, think it means that soul is body—means death for the soul. But the poet knows it means body is soul—the great whole imperishable; in life and in death continually changing substance, always retaining identity. For, if the man of science is happy about the atoms, if he is not baulked or baffled by apparent decay or destruction, but can see far enough into the dimness to know that not only is each atom imperishable, but that its endowments, characteristics, affinities, electric and other attractions and repulsions—however suspended, hid, dormant, masked, when it enters into new combinations—remain unchanged, be it for thousands of years, and, when it is again set free, manifest themselves in the old way, shall not the poet be happy about the vital whole? shall the highest force, the vital, that controls and compels into complete subservience for its own purposes the rest, be the only one that is destructible? and the love and thought that endow the whole be less enduring than the gravitating, chemical, electric powers that endow its atoms? But identity is the essence of love and thought—I still I, you still you. Certainly no man need ever again be scared by the "dark hush" and the little handful of refuse.

"You are not scattered to the winds—you gather certainly and safely around yourself."
"Sure as Life holds all parts together, Death holds all parts together."
"All goes onward and outward: nothing collapses."
"What I am, I am of my body; and what I shall be, I shall be of my body."
"The body parts away at last for the journeys of the soul."

Science knows that whenever a thing passes from a solid to a subtle air, power is set free to a wider scope of action. The poet knows it too, and is dazzled as he turns his eyes toward "the superb vistas of death." He knows that "the perpetual transfers and promotions" and "the amplitude of time" are for a man as well as for the earth. The man of science, with unwearied, self-denying toil, finds the letters and joins them into words. But the poet alone can make complete sentences. The man of science furnishes the premises; but it is the poet who draws the final conclusion. Both together are "swiftly and surely preparing a future greater than all the past." But, while the man of science bequeaths to it the fruits of his toil, the poet, this mighty poet, bequeaths himself—"Death making him really undying." He will "stand as nigh as the nighest" to these men and women. For he taught them, in words which breathe out his very heart and soul into theirs, that "love of comrades" which, like the "soft-born measureless light," makes wholesome and fertile every spot it penetrates to, lighting up dark social and political problems, and kindling into a genial glow that great heart of justice which is the life-source of Democracy. He, the beloved friend of all, initiated for them a "new and superb friendship"; whispered that secret of a godlike pride in a man's self, and a perfect trust in woman, whereby their love for each other, no longer poisoned and stifled, but basking in the light of God's smile, and sending up to him a perfume of gratitude, attains at last a divine and tender completeness. He gave a faith-compelling utterance to that "wisdom which is the certainty of the reality and immortality of things, and of the excellence of things." Happy America, that he should be her son! One sees, indeed, that only a young giant of a nation could produce this kind of greatness, so full of the ardour, the elasticity, the inexhaustible vigour and freshness, the joyousness, the audacity of youth. But I, for one, cannot grudge anything to America. For, after all, the young giant is the old English giant—the great English race renewing its youth in that magnificent land, "Mexican-breathed, Arctic-braced," and girding up its loins to start on a new career that shall match with the greatness of the new home.

A CONFESSION OF FAITH[2]

"Of genius in the Fine Arts," wrote Wordsworth, "the only infallible sign is the widening the sphere of human sensibility for the delight, honour, and benefit of human nature. Genius is the introduction of a new element into the intellectual universe, or, if that be not allowed, it is the application of powers to objects on which they had not before been exercised, or the employment of them in such a manner as to produce effects hitherto unknown. What is all this but an advance or conquest made by the soul of the poet? Is it to be supposed that the reader can make progress of this kind like an Indian prince or general stretched on his palanquin and borne by slaves? No; he is invigorated and inspirited by his leader in order that he may exert himself, for he cannot proceed in quiescence, he cannot be carried like a dead weight. Therefore to create taste is to call forth and bestow power."

A great poet, then, is "a challenge and summons"; and the question first of all is not whether we like or dislike him, but whether we are capable of meeting that challenge, of stepping out of our habitual selves to answer that summons. He works on Nature's plan: Nature, who teaches nothing but supplies infinite material to learn from; who never preaches but drives home her meanings by the resistless eloquence of effects. Therefore the poet makes greater demands upon his reader than any other man. For it is not a question of swallowing his ideas or admiring his handiwork merely, but of seeing, feeling, enjoying, as he sees, feels, enjoys. "The messages of great poems to each man and woman are," says Walt Whitman, "come to us on equal terms, only then can you understand us. We are no better than you; what we enclose you enclose, what we enjoy you may enjoy"—no better than you potentially, that is; but if you would understand us the potential must become the actual, the dormant sympathies must awaken and broaden, the dulled perceptions clear themselves and let in undreamed of delights, the wonder-working imagination must respond, the ear attune itself, the languid soul inhale large draughts of love and hope and courage, those "empyreal airs" that vitalize the poet's world. No wonder the poet is long in finding his audience; no wonder he has to abide the "inexorable tests of Time," which, if indeed he be great, slowly turns the handful into hundreds, the hundreds into thousands, and at last having done its worst, grudgingly passes him on into the ranks of the Immortals.

Meanwhile let not the handful who believe that such a destiny awaits a man of our time cease to give a reason for the faith that is in them.

So far as the suffrages of his own generation go Walt Whitman may, like Wordsworth, tell of the "love, the admiration, the indifference, the slight, the aversion, and even the contempt" with which his poems have been received; but the love and admiration are from even a smaller number, the aversion, the contempt more vehement, more universal and persistent than Wordsworth ever encountered. For the American is a more daring innovator; he cuts loose from precedent, is a very Columbus who has sailed forth alone on perilous seas to seek new shores, to seek a new world for the soul, a world that shall give scope and elevation and beauty to the changed and changing events, aspirations, conditions of modern life. To new aims, new methods; therefore let not the reader approach these poems as a judge, comparing, testing, measuring by what has gone before, but as a willing learner, an unprejudiced seeker for whatever may delight and nourish and exalt the soul. Neither let him be abashed nor daunted by the weight of adverse opinion, the contempt and denial which have been heaped upon the great American even though it be the contempt and denial of the capable, the cultivated, the recognized authorities; for such is the usual lot of the pioneer in whatever field. In religion it is above all to the earnest and conscientious believer that the Reformer has appeared a blasphemer, and in the world of literature it is equally natural that the most careful student, that the warmest lover of the accepted masterpieces, should be the most hostile to one who forsakes the methods by which, or at any rate, in company with which, those triumphs have been achieved. "But," said the wise Goethe, "I will listen to any man's convictions; you may keep your doubts, your negations to yourself, I have plenty of my own." For heartfelt convictions are rare things.

Therefore I make bold to indicate the scope and source of power in Walt Whitman's writings, starting from no wider ground than their effect upon an individual mind. It is not criticism I have to offer; least of all any discussion of the question of form or formlessness in these poems, deeply convinced as I am that when great meanings and great emotions are expressed with corresponding power, literature has done its best, call it what you please. But my aim is rather to suggest such trains of thought, such experience of life as having served to put me *en rapport* with this poet may haply find here and there a reader who is thereby helped to the same end. Hence I quote just as freely from the prose (especially from "Democratic Vistas" and the preface to the first issue of "Leaves of Grass," 1855) as from his poems, and more freely, perhaps, from those parts that have proved a stumbling-block than from those whose conspicuous beauty assures them acceptance.

Fifteen years ago, with feelings partly of indifference, partly of antagonism—for I had heard none but ill words of them—I first opened Walt Whitman's poems. But as I read I became conscious of receiving the most powerful influence that had ever come to me from any source. What was the spell? It was that in them humanity has, in a new sense, found itself; for the first time has dared to accept itself without disparagement, without reservation. For the first time an unrestricted faith in all that is and in the issues of all that happens has burst forth triumphantly into song.

"... The rapture of the hallelujah sent
From all that breathes and is ..."

rings through these poems. They carry up into the region of Imagination and Passion those vaster and more profound conceptions of the universe and of man reached by centuries of that indomitably patient organized search for knowledge, that "skilful cross-questioning of things" called science.

"O truth of the earth I am determined to press my way
    toward you.
Sound your voice! I scale the mountains, I dive in the sea
    after you,"

cried science; and the earth and the sky have answered, and continue inexhaustibly to answer her appeal. And now at last the day dawns which Wordsworth prophesied of: "The man of science," he wrote, "seeks truth as a remote and unknown benefactor; he cherishes and loves it in his solitude. The Poet, singing a song in which all human beings join with him, rejoices in the presence of truth as our visible friend and hourly companion. Poetry is the breath and finer spirit of all knowledge; it is the impassioned expression which is in the countenance of all science, it is the first and last of all knowledge; it is immortal as the heart of man. If the labours of men of science should ever create any material revolution, direct or indirect, in our condition, and in the impressions which we habitually receive, the Poet will then sleep no more than at present; he will be ready to follow the steps of the man of science not only in those general indirect effects, but he will be at his side carrying sensation into the midst of the objects of science itself. If the time should ever come when what is now called science, thus familiarized to man, shall be ready to put on, as it were, a form of flesh and blood, the Poet will lend his divine spirit to aid the transfiguration, and will welcome the being thus produced as a dear and genuine inmate of the household of man." That time approaches: a new heaven and a new earth await us when the knowledge grasped by science is realized, conceived as a whole, related to the world within us by the shaping spirit of imagination. Not in vain, already, for this Poet have they pierced the darkness of the past, and read here and there a word of the earth's history before human eyes beheld it; each word of infinite significance, because involving in it secrets of the whole. A new anthem of the slow, vast, mystic dawn of life he sings in the name of humanity.

"I am an acme of things accomplish'd, and I am an encloser
        of things to be.

"My feet strike an apex of the apices of the stairs;
On every step bunches of ages, and larger bunches between
        the steps;
All below duly travell'd and still I mount and mount.

"Rise after rise bow the phantoms behind me:
Afar down I see the huge first Nothing—I know
I was even there;
I waited unseen and always, and slept through the lethargic
        mist,
And took my time, and took no hurt from the fetid carbon.

"Long I was hugg'd close—long and long.

"Immense have been the preparations for me,
Faithful and friendly the arms that have help'd me.
Cycles ferried my cradle, rowing and rowing like cheerful
        boatmen;
For room to me stars kept aside in their own rings,
They sent influences to look after what was to hold me.

"Before I was born out of my mother, generations guided
    me;
My embryo has never been torpid—nothing could overlay
    it.

"For it the nebula cohered to an orb,
The long slow strata piled to rest it on,
Vast vegetables gave it sustenance,
Monstrous sauroids transported it in their mouths and
    deposited it with care.

"All forces have been steadily employ'd to complete and
    delight me;
Now on this spot I stand with my robust Soul."

    Not in vain have they pierced space as well as time and found
"a vast similitude interlocking all."

"I open my scuttle at night and see the far-sprinkled
    systems,
And all I see, multiplied as high as I can cypher, edge but
    the rim of the farther systems.

"Wider and wider they spread, expanding, always
    expanding,
Outward, and outward, and for ever outward.

"My sun has his sun, and round him obediently wheels,
He joins with his partners a group of superior circuit,
And greater sets follow, making specks of the greatest inside
    them.

"There is no stoppage, and never can be stoppage;

> If I, you, and the worlds, and all beneath or upon their
>   surfaces, were this moment reduced back to a pallid
>   float, it would not avail in the long run;
> We should surely bring up again where we now stand,
> And as surely go as much farther—and then farther and
>   farther."

Not in vain for him have they penetrated into the substances of things to find that what we thought poor, dead, inert matter is (in Clerk Maxwell's words) "a very sanctuary of minuteness and power where molecules obey the laws of their existence, and clash together in fierce collision, or grapple in yet more fierce embrace, building up in secret the forms of visible things"; each stock and stone a busy group of Ariels plying obediently their hidden tasks.

> "Why! who makes much of a miracle?
> As to me, I know of nothing else but miracles,
>
> "To me, every hour of the light and dark is a miracle,
> Every cubic inch of space is a miracle,
> Every square yard of the surface of the earth is spread with
>   the same, ...
> Every spear of grass—the frames, limbs, organs, of men and
>   women, and all that concerns them,
> All these to me are unspeakably perfect miracles."

The natural *is* the supernatural, says Carlyle. It is the message that comes to our time from all quarters alike; from poetry, from science, from the deep brooding of the student of human history. Science materialistic? Rather it is the current theology that is materialistic in comparison. Science may truly be said to have annihilated our gross and brutish conceptions of matter, and to have revealed it to us as subtle, spiritual, energetic beyond our powers of realization. It is for the Poet to increase these powers of realization. He it is who must awaken us to the perception of a new heaven and a new earth here where we stand on this old earth. He it is who must, in Walt Whitman's words, indicate the path between reality and the soul.

Above all is every thought and feeling in these poems touched by the light of the great revolutionary truth that man, unfolded through vast stretches of time out of lowly antecedents, is a rising, not a fallen creature; emerging slowly from purely animal life; as slowly as the strata are piled and the ocean beds hollowed; whole races still barely emerged, countless individuals in the foremost races barely emerged: "the wolf, the snake, the hog" yet lingering in the best; but new ideals achieved, and others come in sight, so that what once seemed fit is fit no longer, is adhered to uneasily and with shame; the conflicts and antagonisms between what we call good and evil, at once the sign and the means of emergence, and needing to account for them no supposed primeval disaster, no outside power thwarting and marring the Divine handiwork, the perfect fitness to its time and place of all that has proceeded from the Great Source. In a word that Evil is relative; is that which the slowly developing reason and conscience bid us leave behind. The prowess of the lion, the subtlety of the fox, are cruelty and duplicity in man.

> "Silent and amazed, when a little boy,
> I remember I heard the preacher every Sunday put God in
>   his statements,
> As contending against some being or influence."

says the poet. And elsewhere, "Faith, very old now, scared away by science"—by the daylight science lets in upon our miserable, inadequate, idolatrous conceptions of God and of His works, and on the sophistications, subterfuges, moral impossibilities, by which we have endeavoured to reconcile the irreconcilable— the coexistence of omnipotent Goodness and an absolute Power of Evil—"Faith must be brought back by the same power that caused her departure: restored with new sway, deeper, wider, higher than ever." And what else, indeed, at bottom, is science so busy at? For what is Faith? "Faith," to borrow venerable and unsurpassed words, "is the substance of things hoped for, the evidence of things not seen." And how obtain evidence of things not seen but by a knowledge of things seen? And how know what we may hope for, but by knowing the truth of what is, here and now? For seen and unseen are parts of the Great Whole: all the parts interdependent, closely related; all alike have proceeded from and are manifestations of the Divine Source. Nature is not the barrier between us and the unseen but the link, the communication; she, too, has something behind appearances, has an unseen soul; she, too, is made of "innumerable energies." Knowledge is not faith, but it is faith's indispensable preliminary and starting ground. Faith runs ahead to fetch glad tidings for us; but if she start from a basis of ignorance and illusion, how can she but run in the wrong direction? "Suppose," said that impetuous lover and seeker of truth, Clifford, "Suppose all moving things to be suddenly stopped at some instant, and that we could be brought fresh, without any previous knowledge, to look at the petrified scene. The spectacle would be immensely absurd. Crowds of people would be senselessly standing on one leg in the street looking at one another's backs; others would be wasting their time by sitting in a train in a place difficult to get at, nearly all with their mouths open, and their bodies in some contorted, unrestful posture. Clocks would stand with their pendulums on one side. Everything would be disorderly, conflicting, in its wrong place. But once remember that the world is in motion, is going somewhere, and everything will be accounted for and found just as it should be. Just so great a change of view, just so complete an explanation is given to us when we recognize that the nature of man and beast and of all the world is *going somewhere.* The maladaptions in organic nature are seen to be steps toward the improvement or discarding of imperfect organs. The *baneful strife which lurketh inborn in us, and goeth on the way with us to hurt us*, is found to be the relic of a time of savage or even lower condition." "Going somewhere!" That is the meaning then of all our perplexities! That changes a mystery which stultified and contradicted the best we knew into a mystery which teaches, allures, elevates; which harmonizes what we know with what we hope. By it we begin to

"... see by the glad light,
And breathe the sweet air of futurity."

The scornful laughter of Carlyle as he points with one hand to the baseness, ignorance, folly, cruelty around us, and with the other to the still unsurpassed poets, sages, heroes, saints of antiquity, whilst he utters the words "progress of the species!" touches us no longer when we have begun to realize "the amplitude of time"; when we know something of the scale by which Nature measures out the years to accomplish her smallest essential modification or development; know that to call a few thousands or tens of thousands of years antiquity, is to speak as a child, and that in her chronology the great days of Egypt and Syria, of Greece and Rome are affairs of yesterday.

"Each of us inevitable;
Each of us limitless—each of us with his or her right upon
    the earth;
Each of us allow'd the eternal purports of the earth;
Each of us here as divinely as any are here.

"You Hottentot with clicking palate! You woolly hair'd
    hordes!
You own'd persons, dropping sweat-drops or blood-drops!
You human forms with the fathomless ever-impressive
    countenances of brutes!
I dare not refuse you—the scope of the world, and of time
    and space are upon me.

"I do not prefer others so very much before you either;
I do not say one word against you, away back there, where
    you stand;
(You will come forward in due time to my side.)
My spirit has pass'd in compassion and determination
    around the whole earth;
I have look'd for equals and lovers, and found them ready
    for me in all lands;
I think some divine rapport has equalized me with them.

"O vapours! I think I have risen with you, and moved away
    to distant continents and fallen down there, for reasons;
I think I have blown with you, O winds;
O waters, I have finger'd every shore with you.

"I have run through what any river or strait of the globe has
    run through;
I have taken my stand on the bases of peninsulas, and on
    the high embedded rocks, to cry thence.

"*Salut au monde!*
What cities the light or warmth penetrates, I penetrate
    those cities myself;
All islands to which birds wing their way I wing my way
    myself.

"Toward all,
I raise high the perpendicular hand—I make the signal,
To remain after me in sight forever,
For all the haunts and homes of men."

But "Hold!" says the reader, especially if he be one who loves
science, who loves to feel the firm ground under his feet, "That
the species has a great future before it we may well believe;
already we see the indications. But that the individual has is

quite another matter. We can but balance probabilities here, and the probabilities are very heavy on the wrong side; the poets must throw in weighty matter indeed to turn the scale the other way!" Be it so: but ponder a moment what science herself has to say bearing on this theme; what are the widest, deepest facts she has reached down to. Indestructibility: Amidst ceaseless change and seeming decay all the elements, all the forces (if indeed they be not one and the same) which operate and substantiate those changes, imperishable; neither matter nor force capable of annihilation. Endless transformations, disappearances, new combinations, but diminution of the total amount never; missing in one place or shape to be found in another, disguised ever so long, ready always to re-emerge. "A particle of oxygen," wrote Faraday, "is ever a particle of oxygen; nothing can in the least wear it. If it enters into combination and disappears as oxygen, if it pass through a thousand combinations, animal, vegetable, mineral—if it lie hid for a thousand years and then be evolved, it is oxygen with its first qualities neither more nor less." So then out of the universe is no door. Continuity again is one of Nature's irrevocable words; everything the result and outcome of what went before; no gaps, no jumps; always a connecting principle which carries forward the great scheme of things as a related whole, which subtly links past and present, like and unlike. Nothing breaks with its past. "It is not," says Helmholtz, "the definite mass of substance which now constitutes the body to which the continuance of the individual is attached. Just as the flame remains the same in appearance and continues to exist with the same form and structure although it draws every moment freshcombustible vapour and fresh oxygen from the air into the vortex of its ascending current; and just as the wave goes on in unaltered form and is yet being reconstructed every moment from fresh particles of water, so is it also in the living being. For the material of the body like that of flame is subject to continuous and comparatively rapid change—a change the more rapid the livelier the activity of the organs in question. Some constituents are renewed from day to day, some from month to month, and others only after years. That which continues to exist as a particular individual is, like the wave and the flame, only the *form of motion* which continually attracts fresh matter into its vortex and expels the old. The observer with a deaf ear recognizes the vibration of sound as long as it is visible and can be felt, bound up with other heavy matter. Are our senses in reference to life like the deaf ear in this respect?"

"You are not thrown to the winds—you gather certainly and
　　safely around yourself;

It is not to diffuse you that you were born of your mother
　　and father—it is to identify you;
It is not that you should be undecided, but that you should
　　be decided;
Something long preparing and formless is arrived and
　　form'd in you,
You are henceforth secure, whatever comes or goes.

"O Death! the voyage of Death!
The beautiful touch of Death, soothing and benumbing a
　　few moments for reasons;
Myself discharging my excrementitious body to be burn'd
　　or reduced to powder or buried.
My real body doubtless left me for other spheres,
My voided body, nothing more to me, returning to the
　　purifications, farther offices, eternal uses of the earth."
Yes, they go their way, those dismissed atoms with all their energies and affinities unimpaired. But they are not all; the will, the affections, the intellect are just as real as those affinities and energies, and there is strict account of all; nothing slips through; there is no door out of the universe. But they are qualities of a personality, of a self, not of an atom but of what uses and dismisses those atoms. If the qualities are indestructible so must the self

be. The little heap of ashes, the puff of gas, do you pretend that is all that was Shakespeare? The rest of him lives in his works, you say? But he lived and was just the same man after those works were produced. The world gained, but he lost nothing of himself, rather grew and strengthened in the production of them.

Still farther, those faculties with which we seek for knowledge are only a part of us, there is something behind which wields them, something that those faculties cannot turn themselves in upon and comprehend; for the part cannot compass the whole. Yet there it is with the irrefragable proof of consciousness. Who should be the mouthpiece of this whole? Who but the poet, the man most fully "possessed of his own soul," the man of the largest consciousness; fullest of love and sympathy which gather into his own life the experiences of others, fullest of imagination; that quality whereof Wordsworth says that it

"... in truth
Is but another name for absolute power,
And clearest insight, amplitude of mind
And reason in her most exalted mood."

Let Walt Whitman speak for us:

"And I know I am solid and sound;
To me the converging objects of the universe perpetually
    flow:
All are written to me, and I must get what the writing
    means.

"I know I am deathless;
I know this orbit of mine cannot be swept by the carpenter's
    compass;
I know I shall not pass like a child's carlacue cut with a
    burnt stick at night.

"I know I am august;
I do not trouble my spirit to vindicate itself or be
    understood;
I see that the elementary laws never apologize;
(I reckon I behave no prouder than the level I plant my
    house by, after all.)

"I exist as I am—that is enough;
If no other in the world be aware I sit content;
And if each one and all be aware, I sit content.

"One world is aware, and by far the largest to me, and that
    is myself;
And whether I come to my own to-day, or in ten thousand
    or ten million years,
I can cheerfully take it now, or with equal cheerfulness I
    can wait.

"My foothold is tenon'd and mortis'd in granite;
I laugh at what you call dissolution;
And I know the amplitude of time."

What lies through the portal of death is hidden from us; but
the laws that govern that unknown land are not all hidden from
us, for they govern here and now; they are immutable, eternal.

"Of and in all these things
I have dream'd that we are not to be changed so much, nor
    the law of us changed,
I have dream'd that heroes and good doers shall be under
    the present and past law,
And that murderers, drunkards, liars, shall be under the
    present and past law,
For I have dream'd that the law they are under now is
    enough."

And the law not to be eluded is the law of consequences, the law of silent teaching. That is the meaning of disease, pain, remorse. Slow to learn are we; but success is assured with limitless Beneficence as our teacher, with limitless time as our opportunity. Already we begin—

"To know the Universe itself as a road—as many roads
As roads for travelling souls.
For ever alive; for ever forward.
Stately, solemn, sad, withdrawn, baffled, mad, turbulent,
    feeble, dissatisfied;
Desperate, proud, fond, sick;
Accepted by men, rejected by men.
They go! they go! I know that they go, but I know not where
    they go.
But I know they go toward the best, toward something
    great;
The whole Universe indicates that it is good."

Going somewhere! And if it is impossible for us to see whither, as in the nature of things it must be, how can we be adequate judges of the way? how can we but often grope and be full of perplexity? But we know that a smooth path, a paradise of a world, could only nurture fools, cowards, sluggards. "Joy is the great unfolder," but pain is the great enlightener, the great stimulus in certain directions, alike of man and beast. How else could the self-preserving instincts, and all that grows out of them, have been evoked? How else those wonders of the moral world, fortitude, patience, sympathy? And if the lesson be too hard comes Death, come "the sure-enwinding arms of Death" to end it, and speed us to the unknown land.

"... Man is only weak
Through his mistrust and want of hope,"

wrote Wordsworth. But man's mistrust of himself is, at bottom, mistrust of the central Fount of power and goodness whence he has issued. Here comes one who plucks out of religion its heart of fear, and puts into it a heart of boundless faith and joy; a faith that beggars previous faiths because it sees that All is good, not part bad and part good; that there is no flaw in the scheme of things, no primeval disaster, no counteracting power; but orderly and sure growth and development, and that infinite Goodness and Wisdom embrace and ever lead forward all that exists. Are you troubled that He is an unknown God; that we cannot by searching find Him out? Why, it would be a poor prospect for the Universe if otherwise; if, embryos that we are, we could compass Him in our thoughts:

"I hear and behold God in every object, yet understand God not in the least."

It is the double misfortune of the churches that they do not study God in His works—man and Nature and their relations to each other; and that they do profess to set Him forth; that they worship therefore a God of man's devising, an idol made by men's minds it is true, not by their hands, but none the less an idol. "Leaves are not more shed out of trees than Bibles are shed out of you," says the poet. They were the best of their time, but not of all time; they need renewing as surely as there is such a thing as growth, as surely as knowledge nourishes and sustains to further development; as surely as time unrolls new pages of the mighty scheme of existence. Nobly has George Sand, too, written: "Everything is divine, even matter; everything is superhuman, even man. God is everywhere. He is in me in a measure proportioned to the little that I am. My present life separates me from Him just in the degree determined by the actual state of childhood of our race. Let me content myself in all my seeking to feel after Him, and to possess of Him as much as this imperfect soul can take in with the intellectual sense I have. The day will come when we shall no longer talk about God idly; nay, when we shall talk about Him as little as possible. We shall cease to set Him forth dogmatically, to dispute about His nature. We shall put compulsion on no one to pray to Him, we shall leave the whole business of worship within the sanctuary of each man's conscience. And this will happen when we are really religious."

In what sense may Walt Whitman be called the Poet of Democracy? It is as giving utterance to this profoundly religious faith in man. He is rather the prophet of what is to be than the celebrator of what is. "Democracy," he writes, "is a word the real gist of which still sleeps quite unawakened, notwithstanding the resonance and the many angry tempests out of which its syllables have come from pen or tongue. It is a great word, whose history, I suppose, remains unwritten because that history has yet to be enacted. It is in some sort younger brother of another great and often used word, Nature, whose history also waits unwritten." Political democracy, now taking shape, is the house to live in, and whilst what we demand of it is room for all, fair chances for all, none disregarded or left out as of no account, the main question, the kind of life that is to be led in that house is altogether beyond the ken of the statesmen as such, and is involved in those deepest facts of the nature and destiny of man which are the themes of Walt Whitman's writings. The practical outcome of that exalted and all-accepting faith in the scheme of things, and in man, toward whom all has led up and in whom all concentrates as the manifestation, the revelation of Divine Power is a changed estimate of himself; a higher reverence for, a loftier belief in the heritage of himself; a perception that pride, not humility, is the true homage to his Maker; that "noblesse oblige" is for the Race, not for a handful; that it is mankind and womankind and their high destiny which constrain to greatness, which can no longer stoop to meanness and lies and base aims, but must needs clothe themselves in "the majesty of honest dealing" (majestic because demanding courage as good as the soldier's, self-denial as good as the saint's for every-day affairs), and walk erect and fearless, a law to themselves, sternest of all lawgivers. Looking back to the palmy days of feudalism, especially as immortalized in Shakespeare's plays, what is it we find most admirable? what is it that fascinates? It is the noble pride, the lofty self-respect; the dignity, the courage and audacity of its great personages. But this pride, this dignity rested half upon a true, half upon a hollow foundation; half upon intrinsic qualities, half upon the ignorance and brutishness of the great masses of the people, whose helpless submission and easily dazzled imaginations made stepping-stones to the elevation of the few, and "hedged round kings," with a specious kind of "divinity." But we have our faces turned toward a new day, and toward heights on which there is room for all.

> "By God, I will accept nothing which all cannot have their
>   counterpart of on the same terms"

is the motto of the great personages, the great souls of to-day. *On the same terms*, for that is Nature's law and cannot be abrogated, the reaping as you sow. But all shall have the chance to sow well. This is pride indeed! Not a pride that isolates, but that can take no rest till our common humanity is lifted out of the mire everywhere, "a pride that cannot stretch too far because sympathy stretches with it":

> "Whoever you are! claim your own at any hazard!
> These shows of the east and west are tame, compared to
>   you;
> These immense meadows—these interminable rivers—
> You are immense and interminable as they;
> These furies, elements, storms, motions of Nature, throes of
>   apparent dissolution—you are he or she who is master
>   or mistress over them,

Master or mistress in your own right over Nature, elements,
  pain, passion, dissolution.

"The hopples fall from your ankles—you find an unfailing
  sufficiency;
Old or young, male or female, rude, low, rejected by the rest,
  whatever you are promulges itself;
Through birth, life, death, burial, the means are provided,
  nothing is scanted;
Through angers, losses, ambition, ignorance and ennui,
  what you are picks its way."

This is indeed a pride that is "calming and excellent to the
soul"; that "dissolves poverty from its need and riches from
its conceit."

And humility? Is there, then, no place for that virtue so much
praised by the haughty? Humility is the sweet spontaneous grace
of an aspiring, finely developed nature which sees always heights
ahead still unclimbed, which outstrips itself in eager longing for
excellence still unattained. Genuine humility takes good care of
itself as men rise in the scale of being; for every height climbed
discloses still new heights beyond. Or it is a wise caution in
fortune's favourites lest they themselves should mistake, as the
unthinking crowd around do, the glitter reflected back upon
them by their surroundings for some superiority inherent in
themselves. It befits them well if there be also due pride, pride of
humanity behind. But to say to a man, 'Be humble' is like saying
to one who has a battle to fight, a race to run, 'You are a poor,
feeble creature; you are not likely to win and you do not deserve
to.' Say rather to him, 'Hold up your head! You were not made
for failure, you were made for victory: go forward with a joyful
confidence in that result sooner or later, and the sooner or the
later depends mainly on yourself.'

"What Christ appeared for in the moral-spiritual field for
humankind, namely, that in respect to the absolute soul there

is in the possession of such by each single individual something so transcendent, so incapable of gradations (like life) that to that extent it places all being on a common level, utterly regardless of the distinctions of intellect, virtue, station, or any height or lowliness whatever" is the secret source of that deathless sentiment of Equality which how many able heads imagine themselves to have slain with ridicule and contempt as Johnson, kicking a stone, imagined he had demolished Idealism when he had simply attributed to the word an impossible meaning. True, *In*equality is one of Nature's words: she moves forward always by means of the exceptional. But the moment the move is accomplished, then all her efforts are toward equality, toward bringing up the rear to that standpoint. But social inequalities, class distinctions, do not stand for or represent Nature's inequalities. Precisely the contrary in the long run. They are devices for holding up many that would else gravitate down and keeping down many who would else rise up; for providing that some should reap who have not sown, and many sow without reaping. But literature tallies the ways of Nature; for though itself the product of the exceptional, its aim is to draw all men up to its own level. The great writer is "hungry for equals day and night," for so only can he be fully understood. "The meal is equally set"; all are invited. Therefore is literature, whether consciously or not, the greatest of all forces on the side of Democracy.

Carlyle has said there is no grand poem in the world but is at bottom a biography—the life of a man. Walt Whitman's poems are not the biography of a man, but they are his actual presence. It is no vain boast when he exclaims,

"Camerado! this is no book;
Who touches this touches a man."

He has infused himself into words in a way that had not before seemed possible; and he causes each reader to feel that he himself or herself has an actual relationship to him, is a reality full of inexhaustible significance andinterest to the poet. The power of his book, beyond even its great intellectual force, is the power with which he makes this felt; his words lay more hold than the grasp of a hand, strike deeper than the gaze or the flash of an eye; to those who comprehend him he stands "nigher than the nighest."

America has had the shaping of Walt Whitman, and he repays the filial debt with a love that knows no stint. Her vast lands with their varied, brilliant climes and rich products, her political scheme, her achievements and her failures, all have contributed to make these poems what they are both directly and indirectly. Above all has that great conflict, the Secession War, found voice in him. And if the reader would understand the true causes and nature of that war, ostensibly waged between North and South, but underneath a tussle for supremacy between the good and the evil genius of America (for there were just as many secret sympathizers with the secession-slave-power in the North as in the South) he will find the clue in the pages of Walt Whitman. Rarely has he risen to a loftier height than in the poem which heralds that volcanic upheaval:—

"Rise, O days, from your fathomless deeps, till you loftier
    and fiercer sweep!
Long for my soul, hungering gymnastic, I devour'd what
    the earth gave me;
Long I roam'd the woods of the north—long I watch'd
    Niagara pouring;
I travel'd the prairies over, and slept on their breast—
I cross'd the Nevadas, I cross'd the plateaus;
I ascended the towering rocks along the Pacific, I sail'd out
    to sea;
I sail'd through the storm, I was refresh'd by the storm;
I watch'd with joy the threatening maws of the waves;

I mark'd the white combs where they career'd so high,
   curling over;
I heard the wind piping, I saw the black clouds;
Saw from below what arose and mounted (O superb! O wild
   as my heart, and powerful!)
Heard the continuous thunder, as it bellow'd after the
   lightning;
Noted the slender and jagged threads of lightning, as
   sudden and fast amid the din they chased each other
   across the sky;
—These, and such as these, I, elate, saw—saw with wonder,
   yet pensive and masterful;
All the menacing might of the globe uprisen around me;
Yet there with my soul I fed—I fed content, supercilious.

"'Twas well, O soul! 'twas a good preparation you gave me!
Now we advance our latent and ampler hunger to fill;
Now we go forth to receive what the earth and the sea never
   gave us;
Not through the mighty woods we go, but through the
   mightier cities;
Something for us is pouring now, more than Niagara
   pouring;
Torrents of men (sources and rills of the Northwest, are you
   indeed inexhaustible?)
What, to pavements and homesteads here—what were those
   storms of the mountains and sea?
What, to passions I witness around me to-day? Was the sea
   risen?
Was the wind piping the pipe of death under the black
   clouds?
Lo! from deeps more unfathomable, something more deadly
   and savage;
Manhattan, rising, advancing with menacing front—
   Cincinnati, Chicago, unchain'd;

—What was that swell I saw on the ocean? behold what
    comes here!
How it climbs with daring feet and hands! how it dashes!
How the true thunder bellows after the lightning! how
    bright the flashes of lightning!
How Democracy, with desperate, vengeful port strides on,
    shown through the dark by those flashes of lightning!
(Yet a mournful wail and low sob I fancied I heard through
    the dark,
In a lull of the deafening confusion.)

"Thunder on! stride on, Democracy! stride with vengeful
    stroke!
And do you rise higher than ever yet, O days, O cities!
Crash heavier, heavier yet, O storms! you have done me
    good;
My soul, prepared in the mountains, absorbs your immortal
    strong nutriment,
—Long had I walk'd my cities, my country roads, through
    farms, only half satisfied;
One doubt, nauseous, undulating like a snake, crawl'd on
    the ground before me,
Continually preceding my steps, turning upon me oft,
    ironically hissing low;
—The cities I loved so well, I abandon'd and left—I sped to
    the certainties suitable to me;
Hungering, hungering, hungering for primal energies, and
    nature's dauntlessness;
I refresh'd myself with it only, I could relish it only;
I waited the bursting forth of the pent fire—on the water
    and air I waited long;
—But now I no longer wait—I am fully satisfied—I am
    glutted;
I have witness'd the true lightning—I have witness'd my
    cities electric;

I have lived to behold man burst forth, and warlike America
　　rise;
Hence I will seek no more the food of the northern solitary
　　wilds,
No more on the mountain roam, or sail the stormy sea."
But not for the poet a soldier's career. "To sit by the wounded
and soothe them, or silently watch the dead" was the part he
chose. During the whole war he remained with the army, but
only to spend the days and nights, saddest, happiest of his life, in
the hospital tents. It was a beautiful destiny for this lover of men,
and a proud triumph for this believer in the People; for it was the
People that he beheld, tried by severest tests. He saw them "of
their own choice, fighting, dying for their own idea, insolently
attacked by the secession-slave-power." From the workshop, the
farm, the store, the desk, they poured forth, officered by men
who had to blunder into knowledge at the cost of the wholesale
slaughter of their troops. He saw them "tried long and long by
hopelessness, mismanagement, defeat; advancing unhesitatingly
through incredible slaughter; sinewy with unconquerable
resolution. He saw them by tens of thousands in the hospitals
tried by yet drearier, more fearful tests—the wound, the
amputation, the shattered face, the slow hot fever, the long
impatient anchorage in bed; he marked their fortitude, decorum,
their religious nature and sweet affection." Finally, newest, most
significant sight of all, victory achieved, the cause, the Union
safe, he saw them return back to the workshop, the farm, the
desk, the store, instantly reabsorbed into the peaceful industries
of the land:—

"A pause—the armies wait.
A million flush'd embattled conquerors wait.
The world, too, waits, then soft as breaking night and sure
　　as dawn
They melt, they disappear."

"Plentifully supplied, last-needed proof of Democracy in its personalities!" ratifying on the broadest scale Wordsworth's haughty claim for average man—"Such is the inherent dignity of human nature that there belong to it sublimities of virtue which all men may attain, and which no man can transcend."

But, aware that peace and prosperity may be even still severer tests of national as of individual virtue and greatness of mind, Walt Whitman scans with anxious, questioning eye the America of to-day. He is no smooth-tongued prophet of easy greatness.

> "I am he who walks the States with a barb'd tongue
>   questioning every one I meet;
> Who are you, that wanted only to be told what you knew
>   before?
> Who are you, that wanted only a book to join you in your
>   nonsense?"

He sees clearly as any the incredible flippancy, the blind fury of parties, the lack of great leaders, the plentiful meanness and vulgarity; the labour question beginning to open like a yawning gulf.... "We sail a dangerous sea of seething currents, all so dark and untried.... It seems as if the Almighty had spread before this nation charts of imperial destinies, dazzling as the sun, yet with many a deep intestine difficulty, and human aggregate of cankerous imperfection saying lo! the roads! The only plans of development, long and varied, with all terrible balks and ebullitions! You said in your soul, I will be empire of empires, putting the history of old-world dynasties, conquests, behind me as of no account—making a new history, a history of democracy ... I alone inaugurating largeness, culminating time. If these, O lands of America, are indeed the prizes, the determinations of your soul, be it so. But behold the cost, and already specimens of the cost. Thought you greatness was to ripen for you like a pear? If you would have greatness, know that you must conquer it through ages ... must pay for it with proportionate price.

For you, too, as for all lands, the struggle, the traitor, the wily person in office, scrofulous wealth, the surfeit of prosperity, the demonism of greed, the hell of passion, the decay of faith, the long postponement, the fossil-like lethargy, the ceaseless need of revolutions, prophets, thunderstorms, deaths, new projections and invigorations of ideas and men."

"Yet I have dreamed, merged in that hidden-tangled problem of our fate, whose long unravelling stretches mysteriously through time—dreamed, portrayed, hinted already—a little or a larger band, a band of brave and true, unprecedented yet, arm'd and equipt at every point, the members separated, it may be by different dates and states, or south or north, or east or west, a year, a century here, and other centuries there, but always one, compact in soul, conscience-conserving, God-inculcating, inspired achievers not only in literature, the greatest art, but achievers in all art—a new undying order, dynasty from age to age transmitted, a band, a class at least as fit to cope with current years, our dangers, needs, as those who, for their time, so long, so well, in armour or in cowl, upheld and made illustrious that far-back-feudal, priestly world."

Of that band, is not Walt Whitman the pioneer? Of that New World literature, say, are not his poems the beginning? A rude beginning if you will. He claims no more and no less. But whatever else they may lack they do not lack vitality, initiative, sublimity. They do not lack that which makes life great and death, with its "transfers and promotions, its superb vistas," exhilarating—a resplendent faith in God and man which will kindle anew the faith of the world:—

"Poets to come! Orators, singers, musicians to come!
Not to-day is to justify me, and answer what I am for;
But you, a new brood, native, athletic, continental, greater
    than before known,

"Arouse! Arouse—for you must justify me—you must
    answer.

"I myself but write one or two indicative words for the
    future,
I but advance a moment, only to wheel and hurry back in
    the darkness.

"I am a man who, sauntering along, without fully stopping,
    turns a casual look upon you, and then averts his face,
Leaving it to you to prove and define it,
    Expecting the main things from you."

Anne Gilchrist.

LETTER I[3]

WALT WHITMAN TO
W. M. ROSSETTI AND ANNE GILCHRIST

Washington,
December 9, 1869.

Dear Mr. Rossetti:

Your letter of last summer to William O'Connor with the
passages transcribed from a lady's correspondence, had been
shown me by him, and copy lately furnished me, which I have
just been rereading. I am deeply touched by these sympathies
and convictions, coming from a woman and from England, and
am sure that if the lady knew how much comfort it has been to
me to get them, she would not only pardon you for transmitting
them to Mr. O'Connor but approve that action. I realize indeed
of this emphatic and smiling *well done* from the heart and
conscience of a true wife and mother, and one too whose sense
of the poetic, as I glean from your letter, after flowing through
the heart and conscience, must also move through and satisfy
science as much as the esthetic, that I had hitherto received no
eulogium so magnificent.

I send by same mail with this, same address as this letter,
two photographs, taken within a few months. One is intended
for the lady (if I may be permitted to send it her)—and will you
please accept the other, with my respects and love? The picture is
by some criticised very severely indeed, but I hope you will not

dislike it, for I confess to myself a perhaps capricious fondness for it, as my own portrait, over some scores that have been made or taken at one time or another.

I am still employed in the Attorney General's office. My p. o. address remains the same. I am quite well and hearty. My new editions, considerably expanded, with what suggestions &c. I have to offer, presented I hope in more definite form, will probably get printed the coming spring. I shall forward you early copies. I send my love to Moncuré Conway, if you see him. I wish he would write to me. If the pictures don't come, or get injured on the way, I will try again by express. I want you to loan this letter to the lady, or if she wishes it, give it to her to keep.

Walt Whitman.

LETTER II

ANNE GILCHRIST TO WALT WHITMAN

September 3, 1871.

Dear Friend:

At last the beloved books have reached my hand—but now I have them, my heart is so rent with anguish, my eyes so blinded, I cannot read in them. I try again and again, but too great waves come swaying up & suffocate me. I will struggle to tell you my story. It seems to me a death struggle. When I was eighteen I met a lad of nineteen[4] who loved me then, and always for the remainder of his life. After we had known each other about a year he asked me to be his wife. But I said that I liked him well as my friend, but could not love him as a wife should love & felt deeply convinced I never should. He was not turned aside, but went on just the same as if that conversation had never passed. After a year he asked me again, and I, deeply moved by and grateful for his steady love, and so sorry for him, said yes. But next day, terrified at what I had done and painfully conscious of the dreary absence from my heart of any faintest gleam of true, tender, wifely love,[5] said no again. This too he bore without desisting & at the end of some months once more asked me with passionate entreaties. Then, dear friend, I prayed very earnestly, and it seemed to me (that) that I should continue to mar & thwart his life so was not right, if he was content to accept what I could give. I knew I could lead a good and wholesome life beside

75

him—his aims were noble—his heart a deep, beautiful, true Poet's heart; but he had not the Poet's great brain. His path was a very arduous one, and I knew I could smooth it for him—cheer him along it. It seemed to me God's will that I should marry him. So I told him the whole truth, and he said he would rather have me on those terms than not have me at all. He said to me many times, "Ah, Annie, it is not you who are so loved that is rich; it is I who so love." And I knew this was true, felt as if my nature were poor & barren beside his. But it was not so, it was only slumbering—undeveloped. For, dear Friend, my soul was so passionately aspiring—it so thirsted & pined for light, it had not power to reach alone and he could not help me on my way. And a woman is so made that she cannot give the tender passionate devotion of her whole nature save to the great conquering soul, stronger in its powers, though not in its aspirations, than her own, that can lead her forever & forever up and on. It is for her soul exactly as it is for her body. The strong divine soul of the man embracing hers with passionate love—so alone the precious germs within her soul can be quickened into life. And the time will come when man will understand that a woman's soul is as dear and needful to his and as different from his as her body to his body. This was what happened to me when I had read for a few days, nay, hours, in your books. It was the divine soul embracing mine. I never before dreamed what love meant: not what life meant. Never was alive before—no words but those of "new birth" can hint the meaning of what then happened to me.

The first few months of my marriage were dark and gloomy to me within, and sometimes I had misgivings whether I had judged aright, but when I knew there was a dear baby coming my heart grew light, and when it was born, such a superb child—all gloom & fear forever vanished. I knew it was God's seal to the marriage, and my heart was full of gratitude and joy. It was a happy and a good life we led together for ten short years, he ever tender and affectionate to me—loving his children so, working earnestly in the wholesome, bracing atmosphere of poverty—for it was but just possible with the most strenuous frugality and industry to pay our way. I learned to cook & to turn my hand to all household occupation—found it bracing, healthful, cheerful. Now I think it more even now that I understand the divineness & sacredness of the Body. I think there is no more beautiful task for a woman than ministering all ways to the health & comfort & enjoyment of the dear bodies of those she loves: no material that will work sweeter, more beautifully into that making of a perfect poem of a man's life which is her true vocation.

In 1861 my children took scarlet fever badly: I thought I should have lost my dear oldest girl. Then my husband took it—and in five days it carried him from me. I think, dear friend, my sorrow was far more bitter, though not so deep, as that of a loving tender wife. As I stood by him in the coffin I felt such remorse I had not, could not have, been more tender to him—such a conviction that if I had loved him as he deserved to be loved he would not have been taken from us. To the last my soul dwelt apart & unmated & his soul dwelt apart unmated. I do not fear the look of his dear silent eyes. I do not think he would even be grieved with me now. My youngest was then a baby. I have had much sweet tranquil happiness, much strenuous work and endeavour raising my darlings.

In May, 1869, came the voice over the Atlantic to me—O, the voice of my Mate: it must be so—my love rises up out of the very depths of the grief & tramples upon despair. I can wait—any time, a lifetime, many lifetimes—I can suffer, I can dare, I can learn, grow, toil, but nothing in life or death can tear out of my heart the passionate belief that one day I shall hear that voice say to me, "My Mate. The one I so much want. Bride, Wife, indissoluble eternal!" It is not happiness I plead with God for—it is the very life of my Soul, my love is its life. Dear Walt. It is a sweet & precious thing, this love; it clings so close, so close to the Soul and Body, all so tenderly dear, so beautiful, so sacred; it yearns with such passion to soothe and comfort & fill thee with sweet tender joy; it aspires as grandly as gloriously as thy own soul. Strong to soar—soft & tender to nestle and caress. If God were to say to me, "See—he that you love you shall not be given to in this life—he is going to set sail on the unknown sea—will you go with him?" never yet has bride sprung into her husband's arms with the joy with which I would take thy hand & spring from the shore.

Understand aright, dear love, the reason of my silence. I was obeying the voice of conscience. I thought I was to wait. For it is the instinct of a woman's nature to wait to be sought—not to seek. And when that May & June I was longing so irrepressibly to write I resolutely restrained myself, believing if I were only patient the right opening would occur. And so it did through Rossetti. And when he, liking what I said, suggested my printing something, it met and enabled me to carry into execution what I was brooding over. For I had, and still have, a strong conviction that it was necessary for a woman to speak—that finally and decisively only a woman can judge a man, only a man a woman, on the subject of their relations. What is blameless, what is good in its effect on her, is good—however it may have seemed to men. She is the test. And I never for a moment feared any hard words against myself because I know these things are not judged by the intellect but by the unerring instincts of the soul. I knew any man could not but feel that it would be a happy and ennobling thing for him that his wife should think & feel as I do on that subject—knew that what had filled me with such great and beautiful thoughts towards men in that writing could not fail to give them good & happy thoughts towards women in the reading. The cause of my consenting to Rossetti's[6] urgent advice that I should not put my name, he so kindly solicitous, yet not altogether understanding me & it aright, was that I did not rightly understand how it might be with my dear Boy if it came before him. I thought perhaps he was not old enough to judge and understand me aright; nor young enough to let it altogether alone. But it has been very bitter & hateful to me this not standing to what I have said as it were, with my own personality, better because of my utter love and faithfulness to the cause & longing to stand openly and proudly in the ranks of its friends; & for the lower reason that my nature is proud and as defiant as thine own and immeasurably disdains any faintest appearance of being afraid of what I had done.

And, my darling, above all because I love thee so tenderly that if hateful words had been spoken against me I could have taken joy in it for thy dear sake. There never yet was the woman who loved that would not joyfully bare her breast to wrest the blows aimed at her beloved.

I know not what fiend made me write those meaningless words in my letter, "it is pleasantest to me" &c., but it was not fear or faithlessness—& it is not pleasantest but hateful to me. Now let me come to beautiful joyous things again. O dear Walt, did you not feel in every word the breath of a woman's love? did you not see as through a transparent veil a soul all radiant and trembling with love stretching out its arms towards you? I was so sure you would speak, would send me some sign: that I was to wait—wait. So I fed my heart with sweet hopes: strengthened it with looking into the eyes of thy picture. O surely in the ineffable tenderness of thy look speaks the yearning of thy man-soul towards my woman-soul? But now I will wait no longer. A higher instinct dominates that other, the instinct for perfect truth. I would if I could lay every thought and action and feeling of my whole life open to thee as it lies to the eye of God. But that cannot be all at once. O come. Come, my darling: look into these eyes and see the loving ardent aspiring soul in them. Easily, easily will you learn to love all the rest of me for the sake of that and take me to your breasts for ever and ever. Out of its great anguish my love has risen stronger, more triumphant than ever: it cannot doubt, cannot fear, is strong, divine, immortal, sure of its fruition this side the grave or the other. "O agonistic throes," tender, passionate yearnings, pinings, triumphant joys, sweet dreams—I took from you all. But, dear love, the sinews of a woman's outer heart are not twisted so strong as a man's: but the heart within is strong & great & loving. So the strain is very terrible. O heart of flesh, hold on yet a few years to the great heart within thee, if it may be. But if not all is assured, all is safe.

This time last year when I seemed dying I could have no secrets between me & my dear children. I told them of my love: told them all they could rightly understand, and laid upon them my earnest injunction that as soon as my mother's life no longer held them here, they should go fearlessly to America, as I should have planted them down there—Land of Promise, my Canaan, to which my soul sings, "Arise, shine, for thy light is come & the glory of the Lord is risen upon thee." After the 29th of this month I shall be in my own home; dear friend—it is at Brookebank, Haslemere, Surrey. Haslemere is on the main line between Portsmouth & London.

Good-bye, dear Walt,

Anne Gilchrist.

Sept. 6.

The new portrait also is a sweet joy & comfort to my longing, pining heart & eyes. How have I brooded & brooded with thankfulness on that one word in thy letter[7] "the comfort it has been to me to get her words," for always day & night these two years has hovered on my lips & in my heart the one prayer: "Dear God, let me comfort him!" Let me comfort thee with my whole being, dear love. I feel much better & stronger now.

LETTER III

_____

ANNE GILCHRIST TO WALT WHITMAN

Brookebank, Shotter Mill
Haslemere, Surrey
October 23, 1871.

Dear Friend:

I wrote you a letter the 6th September & would fain know whether it has reached your hand. If it have not, I will write its contents again quickly to you—if it have, I will wait your time with courage with patience for an answer; but spare me the needless suffering of uncertainty on this point & let me have one line, one word, of assurance that I am no longer hidden from you by a thick cloud—I from thee—not thou from me: for I that have never set eyes upon thee, all the Atlantic flowing between us, yet cleave closer than those that stand nearest & dearest around thee—love thee day & night:—last thoughts, first thoughts, my soul's passionate yearning toward thy divine Soul, every hour, every deed and thought—my love for my children, my hopes, aspirations for them, all taking new shape, new height through this great love. My Soul has staked all upon it. In dull dark moods when I cannot, as it were, see thee, still, still always a dumb, blind yearning towards thee—still it comforts me to touch, to press to me the beloved books—like a child holding some hand in the dark—it knows not whose—but knows it is enough—knows it is a dear, strong, comforting hand. Do not say

I am forward, or that I lack pride because I tell this love to thee who have never sought or made sign of desiring to seek me. Oh, for all that, this love is my pride my glory. Source of sufferings and joys that cannot put themselves into words. Besides, it is not true thou hast not sought or loved me. For when I read the divine poems I feel all folded round in thy love: I feel often as if thou wast pleading so passionately for the love of the woman that can understand thee—that I know not how to bear the yearning answering tenderness that fills my breast. I know that a woman may without hurt to her pride—without stain or blame—tell her love to thee. I feel for a certainty that she may. Try me for this life, my darling—see if I cannot so live, so grow, so learn, so love, that when I die you will say, "This woman has grown to be a very part of me. My soul must have her loving companionship everywhere & in all things. I alone & she alone are not complete identities—it is I and she together in a new, divine, perfect union that form the one complete identity."

I am yet young enough to bear thee children, my darling, if God should so bless me. And would yield my life for this cause with serene joy if it were so appointed, if that were the price for thy having a "perfect child"—knowing my darlings would all be safe & happy in thy loving care—planted down in America.

Let me have a few words directly, dear Friend. I shall get them by the middle of November. I shall have to go to London about then or a little later—to find a house for us—I only came to the old home here from which I have been absent most four years to wind up matters and prepare for a move, for there is nothing to be had in the way of educational advantages here—it has been a beautiful survey for the children, but it is not what they want now. But we leave with regret, for it is one of the sweetest, wildest spots in England, though only 40 miles from London.

Good-bye, dear friend,

Anne Gilchrist.

LETTER IV[8]

WALT WHITMAN TO ANNE GILCHRIST

Washington, D. C.
November 3, 1871.

(To A. G., Earl's Colne, Halsted, Essex, Eng.)

I have been waiting quite a while for time and the right mood, to answer your letter in a spirit as serious as its own, and in the same unmitigated trust and affection. But more daily work than ever has fallen to me to do the present season, and though I am well and contented, my best moods seem to shun me. I wish to give to it a day, a sort of Sabbath, or holy day, apart to itself, under serene and propitious influences, confident that I could then write you a letter which would do you good, and me too. But I must at least show without further delay that I am not insensible to your love. I too send you my love. And do you feel no disappointment because I now write so briefly. My book is my best letter, my response, my truest explanation of all. In it I have put my body and spirit. You understand this better and fuller and clearer than any one else. And I too fully and clearly understand the loving letter it has evoked. Enough that there surely exists so beautiful and a delicate relation, accepted by both of us with joy.

LETTER V

ANNE GILCHRIST TO WALT WHITMAN

27 November '71.

Dear Friend.

Your long waited for letter brought me both joy & pain; but the pain was not of your giving. I gather from it that a long letter[9] which I wrote you Sept. 6th after I had received the precious packet, a letter in which I opened all my heart to you, never reached your hands: nor yet a shorter one[10] which, tortured by anxiety & suspense about its predecessor, I wrote Oct. 15, it, too, written out of such stress & intensity of painful emotion as wrenches from us inmost truth. I cannot face the thought of these words of uttermost trust & love having fallen into other hands. Can both be simply lost? Could any man suffer a base curiosity, to make him so meanly, treacherously cruel? It seems to cut and then burn me.

I was not disappointed at the shortness of your letter & I do not ask nor even wish you to write save when you are inwardly impelled & desirous of doing so. I only want leave and security to write freely to you. Your book does indeed say all—book that is not a book, for the first time a man complete, godlike, august, standing revealed the only way possible, through the garment of speech. Do you know, dear Friend, what it means for a woman, what it means for me, to understand these poems? It means for her whole nature to be then first kindled; quickened into life through such love, such sympathy, such resistless attraction, that thenceforth she cannot choose but live & die striving to become worthy to share this divine man's life—to be his dear companion, closer, nearer, dearer than any man can be—for ever so. Her soul stakes all on this. It is the meaning, the fulfilment, the only perfect development & consummation of her nature— of her passionate, high, immortal aspirations—her Soul to mate with his for ever & ever. O I know the terms are obdurate—I know how hard to attain to this greatness, the grandest lot ever aspired to by woman. I know too my own shortcomings, faults, flaws. You might not be able to give me your great love yet—to take me to your breast with joy. But I can wait. I can grow great & beautiful through sorrow & suffering, working, struggling, yearning, loving so, all alone, as I have done now nearly three years—it will be three in May since I first read the book, first knew what the word *love* meant. Love & Hope are so strong in me, my soul's high aspirations are of such tenacious, passionate intensity, are so conscious of their own deathless reality, that what would starve them out of any other woman only makes them strike out deeper roots, grow more resolute & sturdy, in me. I know that "greatness will not ripen for me like a pear." But I could face, I could joyfully accept, the fiercest anguish, the hardest toil, the longest, sternest probation, to make me fit to be your mate—so that at the last you should say, "This is the woman I have waited for, the woman prepared for me: this is my dear eternal comrade, wife—the one I so much want." Life has no other meaning for me than that—all things have led up to help prepare me for that. Death is more welcome to me than life if it means that—if thou, dear sailor, thou sailing upon thy endless cruise, takest me on board—me, daring, all with thee, steering for the deep waters, bound where mariner has not yet dared to go: hand in hand with thee, nestled close—one with thee. Ah, that word "enough" was like a blow on the breast to me—breast that often & often is so full of yearning tenderness I know not how to draw my breath. The tie between us would not grow less but more beautiful, dear friend, if you knew me *better*: if I could stand as real & near to you as you do to me. But I cannot, like you, clothe my nature in divine poems & so make it visible to you. Ah, foolish me! I thought you would catch a glimpse of it in those words I wrote—I thought you would say to yourself, "Perhaps this is the voice of my mate," and would seek me a little to make sure if it were so or not. O the sweet dreams I have fed on these three years nearly, pervading my waking moments, influencing every thought & action. I was so sure, so sure if I waited silently, patiently, you would send me some sign: so full of joyful hope I could not doubt nor fear. When I lay dying as it seemed, [I was] still full of the radiant certainty that you would seek me, would not lose [me], that we should as surely find one another there as here. And when the ebb ceased & life began to flow back into me, O never doubting but it was for you. Never doubting but that the sweetest, noblest, closest, tenderest companionship ever yet tasted by man & woman was to begin for us here & now. Then came the long, long waiting, the hope deferred: each morning so sure the book would come & with it a word from you that should give me leave to speak: no longer to shut down in stern silence the love, the yearning, the thoughts that seemed to strain & crush my heart. I knew what that means—"if thou wast not gifted to sing thou wouldst surely die." I felt as if my silence must kill me sometimes. Then when the Book came but with it no word for me alone, there was such a storm in [my] heart I could not for weeks read in it. I wrote that long letter out in the Autumn fields for dearlife's sake. I knew I might, and must, speak then. Then I felt relieved, joyful, buoyant once more. Then again months of heart-wearying disappointment as I looked in vain for a letter-O the anguish at times, the scalding tears, the feeling within as if my heart were crushed & doubled up—but always afterwards saying to myself "If this suffering is to make my love which was born & grew up & blossomed all in a moment strike deep root down in the dark & cold, penetrate with painful intensity every fibre of my being, make it a love such as he himself is capable of giving,

then welcome this anguish, these bitter deferments: let its roots
be watered as long as God pleases with my tears."

Anne Gilchrist.

50 Marquis Road
London
Camden Sqr. N. W.

LETTER VI

ANNE GILCHRIST TO WALT WHITMAN

50 Marquis Road, Camden Sqre.
London, N. W.,
January 24, '72.

Dear Friend:

I send you photographs of my oldest and youngest children, I wish I had some worth sending of the other two. That of myself done in 1850 is a copy of a daguerrotype. The recent one was taken just a week or so before I broke down in my long illness & when I was struggling against a terrible sense of inward prostration; so it has not my natural expression, but I think you will like to have [it] rather than none, & the weather here is too gloomy for there to be any chance of a good one if I were to try again. Your few words lifted a heavy weight off me. Very few they are, dear friend: but knowing that I may give to every word you speak its fullest, truest meaning, the more I brood over them the sweeter do they taste. Still I am not as happy & content as I thought I should be if I could only know my words reached you & were welcome to you,—but restless, anxious, impatient, looking so wistfully towards the letters each morning—above all, longing, longing so for you to come—to come & see if you feel happy beside me: no more this painful struggle to put myself into words, but to let what I am & all my life speak to you. Only so can you judge whether I am indeed the woman capable of rising to the full height of great destiny, of justifying & fulfilling your grand thoughts of women. And see my faults, flaws, shortcomings too, dear Friend. I feel an earnest wish you should do this too that there may be the broad unmovable foundation-rock of perfect truth and candour for our love. I do not fear. I believe in a large all-accepting, because all-comprehending, love, a boundless faith in growth & development—in your judging "not as the judge judges but as the sunshine falling around me." To have you in the midst of us! we clustered round you, shone upon, vivified, strengthened by your presence, surrounding you with an atmosphere of love & cheerful life.

When I wrote to you in Nov. I was in lodgings in London, having just accomplished the difficult task of finding a house for us in London, where rents are so high. And I have succeeded better than I anticipated, for we find this a comfortable, dear, little home—small, indeed, but not so small as to interfere with health or comfort, and at rent that I may safely undertake. My Husband was taken from us too young to be able to have made any provision for his children. I have a little of my own—about £80 a year; & for the rest depend upon my Mother, whose only surviving child I am. And she, by nature generous & self-denying as well as prudent, has never made anything but a pleasure of this & as long as she was able to see to her own affairs, was such a capital manager that she used to spare me about £150 out of an income of £350. But now though she retains her faculties in a wonderful degree for her years (just upon 86), she is no longer able to do this & has put the management of the whole into my hands. And I, feeling that she needs, and ought to have, now an easier scale of expenditure at Colne, have to manage a little more cleverly still to make a less sum serve for us. But I succeed capitally, dear friend—do not want a better home, never get behind hand & find it no hardship, but quite the contrary to have to spend a good deal of time & pains in domestic management. And then, just to help me through at the right moment, dear Percy[11] obtained in November a good opening in some large copper & iron mining & smelting works in South Wales at a salary upon which he can comfortably live; & he likes his work well—writes very cheerfully—lodges in a farmhouse in the midst of grand scenery, within a walk of the sea. So this enables me to give the girls a turn in education, for hitherto they have had hardly any teaching but mine. And I chose this part because there is a capital day school for them handy. And Herby[12] walks in to the best drawing school in London & is very diligent and happy at his work. His bent is unmistakably strong. It was well I have had to be so busy this autumn & winter, dear Walt, for I suffered keenly, sometimes overwhelmingly, through the delay in my letters' reaching you. What caused it? And when did you get the Sept. & Oct. letters & did you get the two copies that I, baffled & almost despairing, sent off in Nov.?

Good-bye, dear Friend.

Annie Gilchrist.

LETTER VII[13]

WALT WHITMAN TO ANNE GILCHRIST

(Washington, D. C.)
Feb. 8 '72.

I send by same mail with this my latest piece copied in a newspaper—and write you just a line. I suppose you only received my former letters (two)—I ought to have written something about your children (described to me in your letter of last summer—[July 23d] which I have just been reading again.) Dear boys and girls—how my heart goes out to them.

Did I tell you that I had received letters from Tennyson, and that he cordially invites me to visit him? Sometimes I dream of coming to Old England, on such visit.—& thus of seeing you & your children——But it is a dream only.

I am still living here in employment in a Government office. My health is good. Life is rather sluggish here—yet not without the sunshine. Your letters too were bright rays of it. I am going on to New York soon, to stay a few weeks, but my address will still be here. I wrote lately to Mr. Rossetti quite a long letter. Dear friend, best love & remembrance to you & to the young folk.

LETTER VIII

ANNE GILCHRIST TO WALT WHITMAN

50 Marquis Rd.
Camden Sq. N. W.
April 12th, '72.

Dear Friend:

I was to tell you about my acquaintanceship with Tennyson, which was a pleasant episode in my life at Haslemere. Hearing of the extreme beauty of the scenery thereabouts & specially of its comparative wildness & seclusion, he thought he would like to find or build a house, to escape from the obtrusive curiosity of the multitudes who flock to the Isle of Wight at certain seasons of the year. He is even morbidly sensitive on this point & will not stir beyond his own grounds from week's end to week's end to avoid his admiring or inquisitive persecutors. So, knowing an old friend of mine, he called on me for particulars as to the resources of the neighbourhood. And I, a good walker & familiar with every least frequent spot of hill & dale for some miles round, took him long ambles in quest of a site. Very pleasant rambles they were; Tennyson, under the influence of the fresh, outdoor, quite unconstrained life in new scenery & with a cheerful aim, shaking off the languid ennuyé air, as of a man to whom nothing has any longer a relish—bodily or mental—that too often hangs about him. And we found something quite to his mind—a coppice of 40 acres hanging on the south side two thirds of the way up a hill some 1000 ft. high so as to be sheltered from the cold & yet have the light, dry, elastic hill air—& with, of course, a glorious outlook over the wooded weald of Sussex so richly green & fertile & looking almost as boundless as the great sweep of sky over it—the South Downs to Surrey Hills & near at hand the hill curving round a fir-covered promontory, standing out very black & grand between him & the sunset. Underfoot too a wilderness of beauty—fox gloves (I wonder if they grow in America) ferns, purple heath &c. &c. I don't suppose I shall see much more of him now I have left Haslemere, though I have had very friendly invitations; for I am a home bird—don't like staying out—wanted at home and happiest there. And I should not enjoy being with them in the grand mansion half so much as I did pic-nicing in the road & watching the builders as we did. It is pleasant to see T—with children—little girls at least—he does not take to boys but one of my girls was mostly on his knee when they were in the room & he liked them very much. His two sons are now both 6 ft. high. I have received your letters of March 20 from Brooklyn: but the one you speak of as having acknowledged the photograph never came to hand—a sore disappointment to me, dear Friend. I can ill afford to lose the long & eagerly watched for pleasure of a letter. If it seems to you there must needs be something unreal, illusive, in a love that has grown up entirely without the basis of personal intercourse, dear Friend, then you do not yourself realize your own power nor understand the full meaning of your own words, "whoso touches this, touches a man"—"I have put my Soul & Body into these Poems." Real effects imply real causes. Do you suppose that an ideal figure conjured up by her own fancy could, in a perfectly sound, healthy woman of my age, so happy in her children, so busy & content, practical, earnest, produce such real & tremendous effect—saturating her whole life, colouring every waking moment—filling her with such joys, such pains that the strain of them has been well nigh too much even for a strong frame, coming as it does, after twenty years of hard work?

Therefore please, dear Friend, do not "warn" me any more—it hurts so, as seeming to distrust my love. Time only can show how needlessly. My love, flowing ever fresh & fresh out of my heart, will go with you in all your wanderings, dear Friend, enfolding you day and night, soul & body, with tenderness that tries so vainly to utter itself in these poor, helpless words, that clings closer than any man's love can cling. O, I could not live if I did not believe that sooner or later you will not be able to help stretching out your arms towards me & saying "Come, my Darling." When you get this will you post me an American newspaper (any one you have done with) as a token it has reached you—& so on at intervals during your wanderings; it will serve as a token that you are well, & the postmark will tell me where you are. And thus you will feel free only to write when you have leisure & inclination—& I shall be spared [the] feeling I have when I fancy my letters have not reached you—as if I were so hopelessly, helplessly cut off from you, which is more than I can stand. We all read American news eagerly too. The children are so well & working on with all their might. The school turns out more what I desire for them than I had ventured to hope.

Good-bye, dearest Friend.

Ann Gilchrist.

LETTER IX

ANNE GILCHRIST TO WALT WHITMAN

50 Marquis Rd.
Camden, Sqre.
June 3d, 1872.

Dear Friend:

The newspapers have both come to hand & been gladly welcomed. I shall realize you on the 26th sending living impulses into those young men, with results not to cease—their kindled hearts sending back response through glowing eyes that will be warmer to you than the June sunshine. Perhaps, too, you will have pleasant talks with the eminent astronomers there. Prof. Young, who is so skilful a worker with that most subtle of tidings from the stars, the spectroscope—always, it seems hitherto bringing word of the "vast similitude that interlocks all," nay, of the absolute identity of the stuff they are made of with the stuff we are made of. The news from Dartmouth that too, is a great pleasure.

It has been what seems to me a very long while since last writing, because it has been a troubled time within & what I wrote I tore up again, believing it was best, wisest so. You said in your first letter that if you had leisure you could write one that "would do me good & you too"; write that letter dear Friend after you have been to Dartmouth[14]—for I sorely need it. Perhaps the letters that I have sent you since that first, have given you a

95

feeling of constraint towards me because you cannot respond to them. I will not write any more such letters; or, if I write them because my heart is so full it cannot bear it, they shall not find their way to the Post. But do not, because I give you more than friendship, think that it would not be a very dear & happy thing to me to have friendship only from you. I do not want you to write what it is any effort to write—do not ask for deep thoughts, deep feelings—know well those must choose their own time & mode—but for the simplest current details—for any thing that helps my eyes to pierce the distance & see you as you live & move to-day. I dearly like to hear about your Mother—want to know if all your sisters are married, & if you have plenty of little nephews & nieces—I like to hear anything about Mr. O'Connor[15] & Mr. Burroughs,[16] towards both of whom I feel as toward friends. (Has Mr. O'Connor succeeded in getting practically adopted his new method of making cast steel? Percy[17] being a worker in the field of metallurgy makes me specially glad to hear about this.) Then, I need not tell you how deep an interest I feel in American politics & want to know if you are satisfied with the result of the Cincinnati Convention & what of Mr. Greely?[18] & what you augur as to his success—I am sure dear friend, if you realize the joy it is to me to receive a few words from you—about anything that is passing in your thoughts & around—how beaming bright & happy the day a letter comes & many days after—how light hearted & alert I set about my daily tasks, it would not seem irksome to you to write. And if you say, "Read my books, & be content—you have me in them," I say, it is because I read them so that I am not content. It is an effort to me to turn to any other reading; as to highest literature what I felt three years ago is more than ever true now, with all their precious augmentations. I want nothing else—am fully fed & satisfied there. I sit alone many hours busy with my needle; this used to be tedious; but it is not so now—for always close at hand lie the books that are so dear, so dear, I brooding over the poems, sunning myself in them, pondering the vistas—all the experience of my past life

& all its aspirations corroborating them—all my future & so far as in me lies the future of my children to be shaped modified vitalized by & through these—outwardly & inwardly. How can I be content to live wholly isolated from you? I am sure it is not possible for any one,—man or woman, it does not matter which, to receive these books, not merely with the intellect critically admiring their power & beauty, but with an understanding responsive heart, without feeling it drawn out of their breasts so that they must leave all & come to be with you sometimes without a resistless yearning for personal intercourse that will take no denial. When we come to America I shall not want you to talk to me, shall not be any way importunate. To settle down where there are some that love you & understand your poems, somewhere that you would be sure to come pretty often—to have you sit with me while I worked, you silent, or reading to yourself, I don't mind how: to let my children grow fond of you—to take food with us; if my music pleased you, to let me play & sing to you of an evening. Do your needlework for you—talk freely of all that occupied my thoughts concerning the children's welfare &—I could be very happy so. But silence with the living presence and silence with all the ocean in between are two different things. Therefore, these years stretch out your hand cordially, trustfully, that I may feel its warm grasp.

Good-bye, my dearest friend.

Annie Gilchrist.

LETTER X

ANNE GILCHRIST TO WALT WHITMAN

50 Marquis Rd.
Camden Sq. London
July 14, '72.

The 3d July was my rejoicing day, dearest Friend,—the day the packet from America reached me, scattering for a while the clouds of pain and humiliation & filling me through & through with light & warmth; indeed I believe I am often as happy reading, as you were writing, your Poems. The long new one "As a Strong Bird" of itself answers the question hinted in your preface & nobly fulfils the promise of its opening lines. We want again & again in fresh words & from the new impetus & standpoint of new days the vision that sweeps ahead, the tones that fill us with faith & joy in our present share of life & work— prophetic of the splendid issues. It does not need to be American born to believe & passionately rejoice in the belief of what is preparing in America. It is for humanity. And it comes through England. The noblest souls the most heroic hearts of England were called to be the nucleus of the race that (enriched with the blood & qualities of other races & planted down in the new half of the world reserved in all its fresh beauty & exhaustless riches to be the arena) is to fulfil, justify, outstrip the vision of the poets, the quenchless aspirations of all the ardent souls that have ever struggled forward upon this earth. For me, the most precious page in the book is that which contains the Democratic

Souvenirs. I respond to that as one to whom it means the life of her Soul. It comforts me very much. You speak in the Preface of the imperious & resistless command from within out of which "Leaves of Grass" issued. This carried with it no doubt the secret of a corresponding resistless power over the reader wholly unprecedented, unapproached in literature, as I believe, & to be compared only with that of Christ. I speak out of my own experience when I say that no myth, no "miracle" embodying the notion of a direct communication between God & a human creature, goes beyond the effect, soul & body, of those Poems on me: & that were I to put into Oriental forms of speech what I experienced it would read like one of those old "miracles" or myths. Thus of many things that used to appear to me incomprehensible lies, I now perceive the germ of truth & understand that what was called the supernatural was merely an inadequate & too timid way of conceiving the natural. Had I died the following year, it would have been the simple truth to say I died of joy. The doctor called it nervous exhaustion falling with tremendous violence on the heart which "seemed to have been strained": & was much puzzled how that could have come to pass. I left him in his puzzle—but it was none to me. How could such a dazzling radiance of light flooding the soul, suddenly, kindling it to such intense life, but put a tremendous strain on the vital organs? how could the muscles of the heart suddenly grow adequate to such new work? O the passionate tender gratitude that flooded my breast, the yearnings that seemed to strain the heart beyond endurance that I might repay with all my life & soul & body this debt—that I might give joy to him who filled me with such joy, that I might make his outward life sweeter & more beautiful who made my inner life so divinely sweet & beautiful. But, dear friend, I have certainly to see that this is not to be so, now: that for me too love & death are folded inseparably together: Death that will renew my youth.

I have had the paper from Burlington[19]—with the details a woman likes so to have. I wish I had known for certain whether you went on to Boston & were enjoying the music there. My youngest boy has gone to spend his holiday with his brother in South Wales & he writes me such good news of Per., that he is "looking as brown as a nut & very jolly"; his home in a "clean airy old farm house half way up a mountain in the midst of wild rough grand scenery, sea in sight near enough to hear the sound of it about as loud as the rustling of leaves"—so the boys will have a good time together, and the girls are going with me for the holiday to their grandmother at Colne. W. Rossetti does not take his till October this year. I suppose it will be long & long before this letter reaches you as you will be gone to California—may it be a time full of enjoyment—full to the brim.

Good-bye, dearest Friend,

Annie Gilchrist.

What a noble achievement is Mr. Stanley's:[20] it fills me with pleasure that Americans should thus have been the rescuer of our large-hearted, heroic traveller. We have just got his letters with account of the five races in Central Africa copied from N. Y. *Herald*, July 29.

LETTER XI

ANNE GILCHRIST TO WALT WHITMAN

50 Marquis Road
Camden Sqre.
Novr. 12, 1872.

My Dearest Friend:

I must write not because I have anything to tell you—but because I want so, by help of a few loving words, to come into your presence as it were—into your remembrance. Not more do the things that grow want the sun.

I have received all the papers—& each has made a day very bright for me.

I hope the trip to California has not again had to be postponed—I realize well the enjoyment of it, & what it would be to California & the fresh impulses of thought & emotion that would shape themselves, melodiously, out of that for the new volume.

My children are all well. Beatrice is working hard to get through the requisite amount of Latin, &c. that is required in the preliminary examination—before entering on medical studies. Percy, my eldest, whom I have not seen for a year, is coming to spend Xmas with us.

Good-bye, dearest Friend.
Annie Gilchrist.

LETTER XII

ANNE GILCHRIST TO WALT WHITMAN

50 Marquis Road
Camden Sq. London
Jan. 31, '73.

Dearest Friend:

Shall you never find it in your heart to say a kind word to me again? or a word of some sort? Surely I must have written what displeased you very much that you should turn away from me as the tone of your last letter & the ten months' silence which have followed seem to express to me with such emphasis. But if so, tell me of it, tell me how—with perfect candour, I am worthy of that—a willing learner & striver; not afraid of the pain of looking my own faults & shortcomings steadily in the face. It may be my words have led you to do me some kind of injustice in thought—I then could defend myself. But if it is simply that you are preoccupied, too busy, perhaps very eagerly beset by hundreds like myself whose hearts are so drawn out of their breasts by your Poems that they cannot rest without striving, some way or other, to draw near to you personally—then write once more & tell me so & I will learn to be content. But please let it be a letter just like the first three you wrote: & do not fear that I shall take it to mean anything it doesn't mean. I shall never do that again, though it was natural enough at first, with the deep unquestioning belief I had that I did but answer a call; that I not only might but ought, on pain of being untrue to the greatest, sweetest instincts & aspirations of my own soul, to answer it with all my heart & strength & life. I say to myself, I say to you as I did in my first letters, "This voice that has come to me from over the Atlantic is the one divine voice that has penetrated to my soul: is the utterance of a nature that sends out life-giving warmth & light to my inward self as actually as the Sun does to my body, & draws me to it and shapes & shall shape my course just as the sun shapes the earth's." "Interlocked in a vast similitude" indeed are these inner & outer truths of our lives. It may be that this shaping of my life course toward you will have to be all inward—that to feed upon your words till they pass into the very substance & action of my soul is all that will be given to me & the grateful, yearning, tender love growing ever deeper & stronger out of that will have to go dumb & actionless all my days here. But I can wait long, wait patiently; know well, realize more clearly indeed that this wingless, clouded, half-developed soul of me has a long, long novitiate to live through before it can meet & answer yours on equal terms so as fully to satisfy you, to be in very truth & deed a dear Friend, a chosen companion, a source of joy to you as you of light & life to me. But that is what I will live & die hoping & striving for. That covers & includes all the aspirations all the high hopes I am capable of. And were I to fall away from this belief it would be a fall into utter blackness & despair, as one for whom the Sun in Heaven is blotted out.

Good-bye, dearest Friend.

Annie Gilchrist.

LETTER XIII

ANNE GILCHRIST TO WALT WHITMAN

50 Marquis Road
Camden Sq. N. W.
May 20th, '73.

My Dearest Friend:

Such a joyful surprise was that last paper you sent me with the Poem celebrating the great events in Spain—the new hopes the new life wakening in the breasts of that fine People which has slumbered so long, weighed down & tormented with hideous nightmares of superstition. Are you indeed getting strong & well again? able to drink in draughts of pleasure from the sights & sounds & perfumes of this delicious time, "lilac time"— according to your wont? Sleeping well—eating well, dear friend?

William Rossetti is coming to see me Thursday, before starting for his holiday trip to Naples. His father was a Neapolitan, so he narrowly escaped a lifelong dungeon for having written some patriotic songs—he fled in disguise by help of English friends & spent the rest of his life here. So this, his first visit to Naples, will be specially full of interest & delight to our friend. He is also in great spirits at having discovered a large number of hitherto unknown early letters of Shelley's. Of modern English Poets Shelley is the one he loves & admires incomparably the most. Perhaps this letter will just reach you on your birthday. What can I send you? What can I tell you but the same old story of a heart fast anchored—of a soul to whom your soul is as the sun & the fresh, sweet air, and the nourishing, sustaining earth wherein the other one breathes free & feeds & expands & delights itself. There is no occupation of the day however homely that is not coloured, elevated, made more cheerful to me by thoughts of you & by thoughts you have given me blent in & suffusing all: No hope or aim or practical endeavour for my dear children that has not taken a higher, larger, more joyous scope through you. No immortal aspiration, no thoughts of what lies beyond death, but centre in you. And in moods of pain and discouragement, dear Friend, I turn to that Poem beginning "Whoever you are holding me now in hand," and I don't know but that that one revives and strengthens me more than any. For there is not a line nor a word in it at which my spirit does not rise up instinctively and fearlessly say—"So be it." And then I read other poems & drink in the draught that I know is for me, because it is for all—the love that you give me on the broad ground of my humanity and womanhood. And I understand the reality & preciousness of that. Then I say to myself, "Souls are not made to be frustrated— to have their greatest & best & sweetest impulses and aspirations & yearnings made abortive. Therefore we shall not be 'carried diverse' forever. This dumb soul of mine will not always remain hidden from you—but some way will be given me for this love, this passion of gratitude, this set of all the nerves of my being toward you, to bring joy & comfort to you. I do not ask the When or the How."

I shall be thinking of your great & dear Mother in her beautiful old age, too, on your birthday—happiest woman in all the world that she was & is: forever sacred & dear to America & to all who feed on the Poems of her Son.

Good-bye, my best beloved Friend.

Annie Gilchrist.

I suppose you see all that you care to see in the way of English newspapers. I often long to send you one when there is anything in that I feel sure would interest you, but am withheld by fearing it would be quite superfluous or troublesome even.

LETTER XIV

ANNE GILCHRIST TO WALT WHITMAN

Earls Colne
Halstead
August 12, 1873.

My Dearest Friend:

The paper has just been forwarded here which tells me you are still suffering and not, as I was fondly believing, already quite emerged from the cloud of sickness. My Darling, let me use that tender caressing word once more—for how can I help it, with heart so full & no outlet but words? My darling—I say it over & over to myself with voice, with eyes so full of love, of tender yearning, sorrowful, longing love. I would give all the world if I might come (but am held here yet awhile by a duty nothing may supersede) & soothe & tend & wait on you & with such cheerful loving companionship lift off some of the weight of the long hours & days & perhaps months that must still go over while nature slowly, imperceptibly, but still so surely repairs the mischief within: result of the tremendous ordeal to your frame of those great over-brimming years of life spent in the Army Hospitals. You see dear Friend, a woman who is a mother has thenceforth something of that feeling toward other men who are dear to her. A cherishing, fostering instinct that rejoices so in tending, nursing, caretaking & I should be so happy it needs must diffuse a reviving, comforting, vivifying warmth around you. Might but these words breathed out of the heart of a woman who loves you with her whole soul & life & strength fulfil their errand & comfort the sorrowful heart, if ever so little—& through that revive the drooping frame. This love that has grown up, far away over here, unhelped by the sweet influences of personal intercourse, penetrating the whole substance of a woman's life, swallowing up into itself all her aspirations, hopes, longings, regardless of Death, looking earnestly, confidently beyond that for its fruition, blending more or less with every thought & act of her life—a guiding star that her feet cannot choose but follow resolutely—what can be more real than this, dear Friend? What can have deeper roots, or a more immortal growing power? But I do not ask any longer whether this love is believed in & welcomed & precious to you. For I know that what has real roots cannot fail to bear real flowers & fruits that will in the end be sweet & joyful to you; and that if I am indeed capable of being your eternal comrade, climbing whereon you climb, daring all that you dare, learning all that you learn, suffering all that you suffer (pressing closest then) loving, enjoying all that you love & enjoy—you will want me. You will not be able to help stretching out your hand & drawing me to you. I have written this mostly out in the fields, as I am so fond of doing—the serene, beautiful harvest landscape spread around—returned once more as I have every summer for five & twenty years to this old village where my mother's family have lived in unbroken succession three hundred years, ever since, in fact, the old Priory which they have inhabited, ceased to be a Priory. My Mother's health is still good—wonderful indeed for 88, though she has been 30 years crippled with rheumatism. Still she enjoys getting out in the sunshine in her Bath chair, & is able to take pleasure in seeing her friends & in having us all with her. Her father was a hale man at 90. These eastern counties are flat & tame, but yet under this soft, smiling, summer sky lovely enough too—with their rich green meadows & abundant golden corn crops, now being well got in. Even the sluggish little river Colne one cannot find fault with, it nourishes such a luxuriant border of wild flowers as it creeps along—& turns & twists from sunshine into shade & from shade into sunshine so as to make the very best & most of itself. But as to the human growth here, I think that more than anywhere else in England perhaps it struggled along choked & poisoned by dead things of the past, still holding their place above ground. Carlyle calls the clergy "black dragoons"—in these rural parishes they are black Squires, making it their chief business to instruct the labourer that his grinding poverty & excessive toil, & the Squire's affluence & ease are equally part of the sacred order of Providence. When I have been here a little I wish myself in London again, dearly as I love outdoor life & companionship with nature. For though the same terrible & cruel facts are there as here, they are not choked down your throat by any one, as a beautiful & perfect ideal. Even in England light is unmistakably breaking through the darkness for the toilers.

I did not see William Rossetti before I came down, but heard he had had a very happy time in Italy & splendid weather all the while. Mr. Conway & his wife are going to spend their holiday in Brittany. Do not think me childish dear friend if I send a copy of this letter to Washington as well as to Camden. I want it so to get to you—long & so long to speak with you—& the Camden one may never come to hand—or the Washington one might remain months unforwarded—it is easy to tear up.

I hope it will find you by the sea shore!—getting on so fast toward health & strength again—refreshed & tranquillized, soul & body.

Good-bye, beloved Friend.

Annie Gilchrist.

LETTER XV[21]

WALT WHITMAN TO ANNE GILCHRIST

I must write
friend once more at
Since I last wrote, clouds have darkened over me, and still
   remain.
On the night of 3d January last I was paralyzed, left side, and
have remained so since. Feb. 19 I lost a dear dear sister, who
died in St. Louis leaving two young daughters. May 23d, my
dear inexpressibly beloved mother died in Camden, N. J. I was
just able to get from Washington to her dying bed & sit there.
I thought I was bearing it all stoutly, but I find it affecting the
progress of my recovery since and now. I am still feeble, palsied
& have spells of great distress in the head. But there are points
more favourable.

I am up & dressed every day, sleep & eat middling well & do
not change much yet, in flesh & face, only look very old.

Though I can move slowly very short distances, I walk with
difficulty & have to stay in the house nearly all the time. As I write
to-day, I feel that I shall probably get well—though I may not.

Many times during the past year have I thought of you & your
children. Many times indeed have I been going to write, but did
not. I have just been reading over again several of this & last year's
letters from you & looking at the pictures sent in the one of Jan.
24, '72. (Your letters of Jan. 24, June 3 & July 14, of last year and
of Jan. 31, and May 20, this year, with certainly one other, maybe
two) all came safe. Do not think hard of me for not writing in
reply. If you could look into my spirit & emotion you would be

entirely satisfied & at peace. I am at present temporarily here at Camden, on the Delaware river, opposite Philadelphia, at the house of my brother, and I am occupying, as I write, the rooms wherein my mother died. You must not be unhappy about me, as I am as comfortably situated as can be—& many things—indeed every thing—in my case might be so much worse. Though my plans are not definite, my intention as far as anything is on getting stronger, and after the hot season passes, to get back to Washington for the fall & winter.

My post office address continues at Washington. I send my love to Percy & all your dear children.

The enclosed ring I have just taken from my finger, & send to you, with my love.

LETTER XVI

ANNE GILCHRIST TO WALT WHITMAN

Earls Colne
Sept. 4, 1873.

I am entirely satisfied & at peace, my Beloved—no words can
say how divine a peace.

Pain and joy struggle together in me (but joy getting the
mastery, because its portion is eternal). O the precious letter,
bearing to me the living touch of your hand, vibrating through
& through me as I feel the pressure of the ring that pressed
your flesh—& now will press mine so long as I draw breath. My
Darling! take comfort & strength & joy from me that you have
made so rich & strong. Perhaps it will yet be given us to see each
other, to travel the last stage of this journey side by side, hand
in hand—so completing the preparation for the fresh start on
the greater journey; me loving and blessing her you mourn, now
for your dear sake—then growing to know & love her in full
unison with you.

I hope you will soon get to the sea—as soon as you are strong
enough, that is—& if you could have all needful care & comfort
& a dear friend with you there. For I believe you would get on
faster away from Camden—& that it tends so to keep the wound
open & quivering to be where the blow fell on you—where every
object speaks of her last hours & is laden with heart-stirring
associations; though I realize, dearest Friend, that in the midst
of the poignant sorrow come immortal sweet moments—

112

communings, rapt anticipations. But these would come the same in nature's great soothing arms by the seashore, with her reviving, invigorating breath playing freely over you. If only you could get just strong enough prudently to undertake the journey. When my eyes first open in the morning, often such tender thoughts, yearning ineffably, pitying, sorrowful, sweet thoughts flow into my breast that longs & longs to pillow on itself the suffering head (with white hair more beautiful to me than the silvery clouds which always make me think of it.) My hands want to be so helpful, tending, soothing, serving my whole frame to support his stricken side—O to comfort his heart—to diffuse round him such warm sunshine of love, helping time & the inborn vigour of each organ that the disease could not withstand the influences, but healthful life begin to flow again through every part. My children send their love, their earnest sympathy. Do not feel anyways called on to write except when inwardly impelled. Your silence is not dumb to me now—will never again cloud or pain, or be misconstrued by me. I can feast & feast, & still have wherewithal to satisfy myself with the sweet & precious words that have now come & with the feel of my ring, only send any old paper that comes to hand (never mind whether there is anything to read in it or not) just as a sign that the breath of love & hope these poor words try to bear to you, has reached you. And just one word literally that, dearest, when you begin to feel you are really getting on—to make me so joyful with the news.

Good-bye, dearest Friend,

Anne Gilchrist.

Back again in Marquis Road.

LETTER XVII

ANNE GILCHRIST TO WALT WHITMAN

50 Marquis Rd.
Camden Sq.
Nov. 3, '73 London

My Dearest Friend:

All the papers have reached me—3 separate packets (with the handwriting on them that makes my heart give a glad bound). I look through them full of interest & curiosity, wanting to realize as I do, in things small as well as things large, my Land of Promise—the land where I hope to plant down my children—so strong in the faith that they, & perhaps still more those that come after them will bless me for that (consciously or unconsciously, it doesn't matter which) I should set out with a cheerful heart on that errand if I knew the first breath I drew on American soil would be my last in life. I searched hopeful for a few words telling of improvement in your health in the last paper. But perhaps it does not follow from there being no much mention that there is no progress. May you be steadily though ever so slowly gaining ground, my Darling! Now that I understand the nature of the malady (a deficient flow of blood to the brain, if it has been rightly explained to me) I realize that recovery must be very gradual: as the coming on of it must have been slow & insidious. And perhaps that, & also even from before the war time with its tremendous strain, emotional & physical, is part of the price paid for the greatness of the Poems & for their immortal destiny—the rapt exaltation the intensity of joy & sorrow & struggle—all that went to give them their life-giving power. For I have felt many times in reading them as if the light and heat of their sacred fire must needs have consumed the vital energies of him in whose breast it was generated, faster then even the most splendid physique could renew itself. For our sakes, for humanity's sake, you suffer now, I do not doubt it, every bit as much as the soldier's wounds are for his country's sake. The more precious, the more tenderly cherished, the more drawing the hearts that understand with ineffable yearnings, for this.

My children all continue well in the main, I am thankful to say, though Beatrice (the eldest girl) looks paler than I could wish and is working her brains too much and the rest of her too little just at present, with the hope of getting through the Apothecaries Hall exam. in Arts next Sept., which involves a good bit of Latin and mathematics. This is all women can do in England toward getting into the medical profession & as the Apoth. Hall certificate is accepted for the preliminary studies at Paris & Zurich, I make no doubt it is also at Philadelphia & New York; so that she would be able to enter on medical studies, the virtual preliminary work, when we come. For she continues steadfastly desirous to win her way into that field of usefulness, & I believe is well fitted to work there, with her grave, earnest, thoughtful, feeling nature & strong bodily frame. She is able to enjoy your Poems & the vistas; broods over them a great deal. Percy is bending his energies now to mastering the processes that go to the production of the very best quality of copper such as is used for telegraph wires &c. No easy matter, copper being the most difficult, in a metallurgical point of view, of all the metals to deal with & the Company in whose employ he is having hitherto been unsuccessful in this branch. His looks, too, do not quite satisfy me—it is partly rather too long hours of work—but still more not getting a good meal till the end of it. It is so hard to make the young believe that the stomach shares the fatigue of the rest of the body and that there is not nervous energy enough left for it to do all its principal work to perfection after a long, exhausting day. But I hope now I, or rather his own experience and I together, have convinced him in time, and he promises me faithfully to arrange for a good meal in the middle of the day however much grudging the time. My little artist Herby is still chiefly working from the antique, but tries his hand at home occasionally with oils & to life & has made an oil sketch of me which, though imperfect in drawing &c., gives far more the real character & expression of my face than the photographs. Have you heard, I wonder, of William Rossetti's approaching marriage? It is to take place early in the New Year. The lady is Lucy Brown, daughter of one of our most eminent artists (he was the friend who first put into my hand the "Selections" from your Poems). Lucy is a very sweet-tempered, cultivated, lovable woman, well fitted, I should say, to make William Rossetti happy. They are to continue in the old home, Euston Sq., with Mrs. Rossetti & the sisters, who are one and all fond of Lucy. I am glad he is going to be married for I think he is a man capable both of giving and receiving a large measure of domestic happiness. I hope the dear little girls at St. Louis are well. And you, my Darling, O surely the sun is piercing through the dark clouds once more and strength & health and gladness returning. O fill yourself with happy thoughts for you have filled others with joy & strength & will do so for countless generations, & from these hearts flows back, and will ever flow, a steady current of love & the beautiful fruits of love.

When you next send me a paper, if you feel that you are getting on ever so little, dearest friend, just a dash under the word *London*. I have looked back at all your old addresses & I see you never do put any lines, so I shall know it was not done absently but really means you are better. And how that line will gladden my eyes, Darling!

Love from us all. Good-bye.
Anne Gilchrist.

LETTER XVIII

___

ANNE GILCHRIST TO WALT WHITMAN

50 Marquis Rd.
Camden Sq., N. W.
Dec. 8, 1873.

My Dearest Friend:

The papers with Prof. Young's speech came safely & I read it, my hand in yours, happy and full of interest. Are you getting on, my Darling? When I know that you no longer suffer from distressing sensations in the head & can move without such effort and difficulty, a hymn of thankfulness will go up from my heart. Perhaps this week I shall get the paper with the line on it that is to tell me so much—or at least that you are well on your way towards it. And what shall I tell you about? The quiet tenor of our daily lives here? but that is very restricted, though, I trust, as far as it goes, good & healthful. O the thoughts and hopes that leap from across the ocean & the years! But they hide themselves away when I want to put them into words. Do not think I live in dreams. I know very well it is strictly in proportion as the present & the past have been busy shaping & preparing the materials of a beautiful future, that it really will be beautiful when it comes to exist as a present, seeing how it needs must be entirely a growth from all that has preceded it & that there are no sudden creations of flowers of happiness in men & women any more than in the fields. But if the buds lie ready folded, ah, what the sunshine will

117

do! What fills me with such deep joy in your poems is the sense of the large complete acceptiveness—the full & perfect faith in humanity—in *every individual unit of humanity*—thus for the first time uttered. That alone satisfies the sense of justice in the soul, responds to what its own nature compels it to believe of the Infinite Source of all. That too includes within its scope the lot as well as the man. His infinite, undying self must achieve and fulfil itself out of any & all experiences. Why, if it takes such ages & such vicissitudes to compact a bit of rock—fierce heat, & icy cold, storms, deluges, crushing pressure & slow subsidences, as if it were like a handful of grass & all sunshine—what would it do for a man!

Dec. 18.

The longed-for paper has come to hand. O it *is* a slow struggle back to health, my Darling! I believe in the main it is good news that is come—and there is the little stroke I wanted so on the address. But for all that, I feel troubled & conscious—for I believe you have been a great deal worse since you wrote—and that you have still such a steep, steep hill to climb.

Perhaps if my hand were in yours, dear Walt, you would get along faster. Dearer and sweeter that lot than even to have been your bride in the full flush & strength and glory of your youth. I turn my face to the westward sky before I lie down to sleep, deep & steadfast within me the silent aspiration that every year, every month & week, may help something to prepare and make fitter me and mine to be your comfort and joy. We are full of imperfections, short-comings but half developed, but half "possessing our own souls." But we grow, we learn, we strive—that is the best of us. I think in the sunshine of your presence we shall grow fast—I too, my years notwithstanding. May the New Year lead you out into the sunshine again—shed out of its days health & strength, so that you tread the earth in gladness again. This with love from us all.

Good-bye, dearest Friend.

Anne Gilchrist.

Herby was at a Conversation last night where were many distinguished men & beautiful women. Among the works of art displayed on the walls was a fine photograph of you.

19th, afternoon.

And now a later post has brought me the other No. of the *Graphic* with your own writing in it—so full of life and spirit, so fresh & cheerful & vivid, dear Friend, it seems to scatter all anxious sad thoughts to the winds. And are you then really back at Washington, I wonder, or have you only visited it in spirit, & written the recollection of former evenings?

I shall have none but cheerful thoughts now. I shall reread it carefully—read it to the young folk at tea to-night.

LETTER XIX

ANNE GILCHRIST TO WALT WHITMAN

50 Marquis Rd.
Camden Sq.
London
26 Feb., 1874.

My Dearest Friend:

Glad am I when the time comes round for writing to you again—though I can't please myself with my letters, poor little echoes that they are of the loving, hoping, far-journeying thoughts so busy within. It has been a happy time since I received the paper with the joyful news you were back at Washington, well on your way to recovery, able partially to resume work—scenting from afar the fresh breeze & sunshine of perfect health—by this time, not from afar, perhaps. The thought of that makes dull days bright & bright days glorious to me too. I note in the New York *Graphic* that a new edition of "Leaves of Grass" was called for— sign truly that America is not so very slowly & now absorbing the precious food she needs above all else? Perhaps, dear Friend, even during your lifetime will begin to come the proof you will alone accept—that "your country absorbs you as affectionately as you have absorbed it." I have had two great pleasures since I last wrote you. One is that Herby has read with a large measure of responsive delight "Leaves of Grass" quite through, so that he now sees you with his own eyes & has in his heart the living, growing germs of a loving admiration that will grow with his growth & strengthen every fibre of good in him. Also he read & took much pride in my "letters," now shown him for the first time. Percy has had a fortnight's holiday with us, and looks better in health, though still not altogether as I could wish. He says he is getting such good experience he would not care just yet to change his post even for better pay. Music is his greatest pleasure—he seems to get more enjoyment out of that than out of literature, & is acquiring some practical skill.

To-day (Feb. 25th) is my birthday, dearest Friend—a day my children always make very bright & happy to me: and on it they make me promise to "do nothing but what I like all day." So I shall spend it with you—partly in finishing this letter, partly reading in the book that is so dear to me—for that is indeed my soul coming into the presence of your soul—filled by it with strength & warmth & joy. In discouraged moods, when oppressed with the consciousness of my own limitations, failures, lack of many beautiful gifts, I say to myself, "What sort of a bird with unfledged wings are you that would mate with an eagle? Can your eyes look the sun in the face like his? Can you sustain your long, lifelong flights upward? Can you rest in dizzy rocks overhanging dark, tempestuous abysses? Is your heart like his, a great glowing sun of Love?" Then I answer, "Give me Time." I can bide my time—a long, long growing & unfolding time. That he draws me with such power, that my soul has found the meaning of itself in him— the object of all its deep, deathless aspirations in comradeship with him, means, if life is not a mockery clean ended by death, that the germs are in me, that through cleaving & loving & ever striving up & on I shall grow like him—like but different—the correlative—what his soul needs & desires; and if when I reach America he is not so drawn towards me,—if seeing how often I disappoint myself, needs must that he too is disappointed, still I can hold bravely, lovingly on to this inextinguishable faith & hope—with the added joy of his presence, sometimes winning from him more & more a dear friendship, yielding him some joy & comfort—for he too turns with hope, with yearning, towards me—bids me be "satisfied & at peace!" So I am, so I will be, my darling. Surely, surely, sooner or later I shall justify that hope, satisfy that yearning. This is what I say to myself & to you this 46th birthday. Have I said it over & over again? That is because it is the undercurrent of my whole life. The *Tribune* with Proctor's "Lecture on the Sun" (& a great deal besides that interests me) came safe. A masterly lecture. And two days ago came the Philadelphia paper with Prof. Morton's speech—deeply interesting. And as I read these things, the feeling that they have come from, & been read by, you turns them into Poems for me.

Good-bye, my dearest Friend.

Anne Gilchrist.

W. Rossetti's marriage is to be the end of next month. Had a pleasant chat with Mr. Conway, who took supper with us a week or two ago.

LETTER XX

ANNE GILCHRIST TO WALT WHITMAN

March 9th, 1874.

With full heart, with eyes wet with tears of joy & I know not what other deep emotion—pain of yearning pity blent with the sense of grandeur—dearest Friend, have I read and reread the great, sacred Poem just come to me.[22] O august Columbus! whose sorrows, sufferings, struggles are more to be envied than any triumph of conquering warrior—as I see him in your poem his figure merges into yours, brother of Columbus. Completer of his work, discoverer of the spiritual, the ideal America—you too have sailed over stormy seas to your goal—surrounded with mocking disbelievers—you too have paid the great price of health—our Columbus.

Your accents pierce me through & through.

Your loving Annie.

LETTER XXI

ANNE GILCHRIST TO WALT WHITMAN

50 Marquis Rd.
Camden Sq.
May 14, 1874.

My Dearest Friend:

Two papers have come to hand since I last wrote, one containing the memoranda made during the war—precious records, eagerly read & treasured & reread by me.

How the busy days slip by one so like another, yet each with its own fresh & pleasant flavour & scent, as like and as different as the leaves on a tree, or the plants in the hedgerows. Days they are busy with humble enough occupations, but lit up for me not only with the light of hope, but with the half-hidden joy of one who knows she has found what she sought and laid such strong hold upon it that she fears nothing, questions nothing—no life, or death, nor in the end, in her own imperfections, flaws, shortcomings. For to be so conscious of these, and to love and understand you so, are proofs [that] the germs of all are in her, & perhaps in the warmth & joyous sunshine of your presence would grow fast. Anyhow, distance has not baffled her, and time will not. A great deal of needlework to be done at this time of year; for my girls have not time for any at present; it is not a good contrast or the right thing after longish hours of study—much better household activity of any sort. If they would but understand this in schools & colleges for girls & young women. No healthier or more cheerful occupation as a relief from study, could be found than household work—sweeping, scrubbing, washing, ironing, cooking—in the variety of it, & equable development of the muscles, I should think equal to the most elaborate gymnastics. I know very well how I have felt, & still feel, the want of having been put to these things when a girl. Then the importance afterwards of doing them easily & well & without undue fatigue, to all who aim to give practical shape to their ardent belief in equality & fair play for all. In domestic life under one roof, at all events, it is already feasible to make the disposals without ignominious distinctions—not all the rough bodily work, never ending, leisure all to the other; but a wholesome interchange and sharing of these. Not least too among the advantages of taking an active share in these duties is the zest, the keen relish, it gives to the hours not too easily secured for reading & music. Besides, I often think that just as the Poem Nature is made up half of rude, rough realities and homely materials & processes, so it is necessary for women to construct their Poem, Home, on a groundwork of homeliest details & occupations, providing for the bodily wants & comforts of their household, and that without putting their own hands to this, their Poem will lack the vital, fresh, growing, nature-like quality that alone endures, and that of this soil will grow, with fitting preparation & culture, noble & more vigorous intellectual life in women, fit to embody itself in wider spheres afterwards—if the call comes.

This month of May that comes to you so laden with great and sorrowful & beautiful & tender memories, and that is your birth-month too, I cannot say that I think of you more than at any other time, for there is no month nor day that my thoughts do not habitually & spontaneously turn to you, refer all to you— yet I seem to come closer because of the Poems that tell me of what relates to that time; but most of all when I think of your beloved Mother, because then I often yearn, more than I know how to bear, to comfort you with love and tender care and silent companionship. May is in a sense (& a very real one) my birth-month too, for in it were your Poems first put into my hand. I wish I were *quite sure* that you no longer suffer in your head, and that you can move about without effort or difficulty—perhaps before long there will be a paper with some paragraph about your health, for though we say to ourselves no news is good news, it is a very different thing to have the absolute affirmation of good news.

My children are all well and hearty, I am thankful to say, & working industriously. Grace means to study the best system of kindergarten teaching—I fancy she is well suited for kindergarten teaching & that it is very excellent work.

Herby is still drawing from the antique in the British Museum. I hope he will get into the Academy this summer. He is going to spend his holidays with his brother in South Wales—and we as usual at Colne, but that will not be till August.

Did I tell you William Rossetti and his bride were spending their honeymoon at Naples? & have found it bitterly cold there, I learn. Mr. & Mrs. Conway & their children are well. Eustace is coming to spend the afternoon with Herby to-morrow.

Good-bye, my dearest Friend.

Annie Gilchrist.

LETTER XXII

ANNE GILCHRIST TO WALT WHITMAN

50 Marquis Rd.
Camden Sq.
July 4, 1874.

My Dearest Friend:

Are you well and happy, and enjoying this beautiful summer? London is, in one sense, a sort of big prison at this time of year: but still at a wide open window, with the blue sky opening to me & a soft breeze blowing in & the Book that is so dear—my life-giving treasure—open on my lap, I have very happy times. No one hundreds of years hence will find deeper joy in these poems than I—breathe the fresh, sweet, exhilarating air of them, bathe in it, drink in what nourishes & delights the whole being, body, intellect & soul, more than I. Nor could you, when writing them, have desired to come nearer to a human being & be more to them forever & forever than you are & will be to me. O I take the hand you stretch out each day—I put mine into it with a sense of utter fulfilment: I ask nothing more of time and of eternity but to live and grow up to that companionship that includes all.

6th. This very morning has come the answer to my question. First I only saw the Poem—read it so elate—soared with it to joyous heights, said to myself: "He is so well again, he is able to take the journey into Massachusetts & speak the kindling words." Then I turned over and my joy was dashed. My Darling;

such patience yet needed along the tedious path! Oh, it makes me long, with passionate longings, with yearnings I know not how to bear, to come, to be your loving, cheerful companion, the one to take such care, to do all for you—to beguile the time, to give you of my health as you have done to tens of thousands. I do not doubt, either, but that you will get well. I feel sure, sure, it will be given me to see you; and perhaps a very slow, gradual recovery is safest—is the only way in this as in other matters to thoroughness; & a very speedy rally would be specious, treacherous, in the end, leading you to do what you were not yet fit for. I believe if I could only make you conscious of the love, the enfolding love, my heart breathes out toward you it would do you physical good; many-sided love—Mother's love that cherishes, that delights so in personal service, that sees in sickness & suffering such dear appeals to an answering, limitless tenderness—wife's love—ah, you draw that from me too, resistlessly—I have no choice— comrade's love, so happy in sharing all, pain, sorrow, toil, effort, enjoyments, thoughts, hopes, aims, struggles, disappointment, beliefs, aspirations. Child's love, too, that trusts utterly, confides unquestioningly. Not more spontaneously, & wholly without effort or volition on my part, does the sunlight flow into my eyes when I open them in the morning than does the sense of your existence enter like bright light into my awaking soul. And then I send to you thoughts—tender, caressing thoughts—that would fain nestle so close—ah, if you could feel them, take them in, let them lie in your breast, each morning.

My children are all well, dear Friend. Herbert is going to spend his holidays with his brother in Wales—& we shall all go to Colne as usual the end of this month & remain there through August and September; so if you think of it, address any paper you may send [to] Earls Colne, Halstead, because I should get it a day sooner. But it does not signify if you forget & send it here; it will be forwarded all right. Beatrice has just got through one of the Govern. Exams. in elementary mathematics; and I hope Herby has got into the Academy, but do not know for certain yet. He works away zealously and with great delight in his work. William Rossetti and his wife are coming to dine with us Wednesday— they look so well and happy, it does one good to see them. The Conways are going to Ostend, I think, for their holiday, & when they come back [are] going to move into a larger house. I heard an American lady, Miss Whitman, sing at a concert the other day, who delighted me, fascinated me—I longed to kiss her after each song, though some of them were poor enough Verdi stuff— but she contrived to impart genuineness & beauty to them. I hope you will hear her when she returns to America, which will be soon, I believe.

Good-bye, dearest Friend. Beatrice, Herby & Grace join their love with mine. I had the sweet little Bridal Poem all safe, & by the bye I liked that Springfield paper very much.

Your loving Annie.

LETTER XXIII

ANNE GILCHRIST TO WALT WHITMAN

Earls Colne
Sept. 3, 1874.

My Dearest Friend:

The change down here has refreshed me more than usual and I find my Mother still wonderful for her years (the 89th), able to get out daily in her Bath chair for two or three hours—to enjoy our being with her, and suffering little or no pain from rheumatism now. I hope you have had as glorious a summer & harvest as we have, and that you are able to be much out of doors and absorb the health-giving influences, dear Friend. Such mornings! So fresh and invigourating. I have been before breakfast mostly in a beautiful garden (the old Priory garden) with my beloved Poems and the dew-laden flowers and liquid light and sweet, fresh air; & the sparkle of the pond & delicious greenness of the meadows beyond & rustling trees, and had a joyful time with you, my Darling—sometimes with thoughts that lay hold on "the solid prizes of the Universe," sometimes so busy building up a home in America, thinking, dreaming, hoping, loving, groping among dim shadows, straining wistful eyes into the dim distance—then to my poems again—ah! not groping then, but hand in hand with you, breathing the air you breathe, with eyes ardently fixed in the same direction your eyes look, heart beating strong with the same hopes, aspirations, yours beats with. It does not need to be American to love America and to believe in the great future of humanity there; it is curious to be human, still more English to do that. I love & believe in & understand her in & through you: but was always drawn towards her, always a believer, though in a vaguer way, that a new glorious day for men & women was dawning there, and recognized a new, distinctive American quality, very congenial to me, even in American virtues, which you not perhaps rate highly or retard as decisively national, not adequately or commandingly so, at any rate. Did I ever tell you the cousin of mine[23] who owns the priory here fought for two years in the Secession war in the army of the Potomac when Burnside & McClellan were at the head? John Cowardine was Major in a Cavalry regiment—was at Vicksburg, Frederickburg, &c. Never wounded, or but slightly—had a good deal of outpost duty, being just the right sort of a man for that, & has letters of approval from his generals of which he is not a little proud. Before that fought under the Stars & Stripes in Mexico & has had a curiously adventurous career, which he commenced by running away from a military college, where he was being prepared for a cadetship, & enlisting as a private—getting out of that by & bye and working his way before the mast as a sailor—then mining in California—then in Australia, riding steeplechases, keeper of the Melrose hounds, market gardening, hotel keeping, then on his way back to California, cast ashore on one of the Navigator Islands, where he remained for six months, the only white man among savages, who were friendly & made much of him—now, come into a good estate, married to a woman who seems to suit him well & is healthy, cheerful rich & handsome, he has fallen into indifferent health & considerable depression of spirits. Perhaps he finds the atmosphere of Squirearchical gentility very stagnant, the bed of roses stifling—perhaps, too, the severe privations he has at different times undergone have injured him. I often think he was perhaps one of those your eyes rested on with pride & admiration—"handsome, tan-faced, dressed in blue." He is the very ideal of a soldier in appearance & bearing—

has now some fine children, of whom he is very fond.

It was just this time of year I received the precious letter and ring that put peace and joy, and yet such pain of yearning, into my heart—pain for you, my Darling. O sorrowing helpless love that waits, and must wait, useless, afar off, while you suffer. But trying every day of my life to grow fitter, more capable of being your comfort and joy and true comrade—never to cease trying this side death or the other—rejoicing in my children more than I ever rejoiced in them before, now that in and through you I for the first time see and understand humanity (myself included)—its divine nature, its possibilities, nay, its certainties. How I do long for you to see my children, dear Friend, and for them to see and love you as they will love you, and all their nature unfold and grow more vigorously and joyously under your influence. Gracie, of whom you have photographs, grows fast,—is such a fine, blooming girl. I hope soon to send you one of Beatrice too. They have been enjoying their visit here and are now gone home. Gracie for school, Beatrice for the examination at Apoth. Hall she is hoping to get through. Then she is coming here to be with my Mother, & I going back to London. We mean now one or other of us always to be with my Mother here. Herby has had such a happy time with his brother in Wales—& is looking as brown as a nut & full of health & life—he had a swim in the sea every day. He did succeed in getting into the Academy, & will begin work there Oct. 1st! Be sure, dear Friend, if there is a word about your health in any paper to send it me—that is what I search for so eagerly—to have the joyful news you are getting on—but even if it is but so very very slowly, still I would rather know the truth? I do not like thinking of you mistakenly. I want to send you the thoughts, the yearnings, that belong to you, the cherishing love that enfolds you most tenderly of all when you suffer. O if I could send it! and the cheerful companionship, beguiling the time while strength creeps back. I hope your little nieces at St. Louis are well.

Good-bye, my dearest Friend. Herby, the only one here with

me, would like to join his love with mine.

Annie Gilchrist.

I go back the beginning of October.
Sep. 14th.

LETTER XXIV

ANNE GILCHRIST TO WALT WHITMAN

50 Marquis Rd.
Camden Sq. London
Dec. 9, 1874.

My Dearest Friend:

It did me much good to get your Poem—beautiful, earnest, eloquent words from the soul whose dear companionship mine seeks with persistent longing—wrestling with distance & time. It seems to me, too, from your having spoken the Poem yourself I may conclude you have made fair progress. What I would fain know is whether you have recovered the use of the left side so far as to get about pretty freely and to have as much open-air life as you need & like; and also whether you have quite ceased to suffer distressing sensations in the head. If you can say yes to the first question, will you in sign of it put a dash under the word *London*, and if yes to the second under *England*, when you next send me a paper? Unless indeed the paper itself contain a notice of your health. But if it does not, that would be an easy way of gladdening me with good news, if good news there is. I wish I could send you good letters, dearest Friend, making myself the vehicle of what is stirring around me in life & thought that would interest you; for there is plenty. But that is very hard to do—though I watch, hear, read eagerly, full of interest. Everything stirs in me a cloud of questions, makes me want to see its relationship to what I hold already. I am forever brooding, pondering, sifting, testing—but that is not the bent of mind that enables one to reproduce one's impressions in compact & lively form. So please, dear Friend, be indulgent, as indeed I know you will be, of these poor letters of mine with their details of my children & their iterated and reiterated expressions of the love and hope and aspiration you have called into life within me—take them not for what they are, but for all they have to stand for. Beatrice is at Colne (having got well through the exam. we were anxious about in the autumn) and is a very great comfort to my Mother—as I well knew she would be; for a more affectionate, devoted, care-taking nature does not breathe—with a strong active mental life of her own too. So, though missing her sorely, I am well satisfied she should be there; and the country life and rest are doing her a world of good. My artist boy is working away cheerily at the R. Academy, his heart in his work. Percy is coming to spend Xmas with us— he, too, continues well content with his work and in good health. Gracie is blooming. The Rossettis have had a heavy affliction this first year of their married life in the premature death of her only brother—a young man of considerable promise—barely 20.

The Conways are well. I feel more completely myself than I have done since my illness—so you see, dear friend, if it has taken me quite four years to recover the lost ground, one must not be discouraged if two do not accomplish it in your case. I hope your little nieces[24] at St. Louis are well—and the brothers you are with, and that you have many dear friends round you at Camden.

I think my thoughts fly to you on strongest and most joyous wings when I am out walking in the clear, cold, elastic air I enjoy so much.

    Good-bye, my dearest Friend.
    Annie Gilchrist.

A cheerful Christmas, a New Year of which each day brings its share of restorative influence, be yours.

LETTER XXV

ANNE GILCHRIST TO WALT WHITMAN

50 Marquis Rd.
Camden Sq.
Dec. 30, 1874.

I see, my dearest Friend, I must not look for those dashes under the words I thought were going to convey a joyful confirmation of my hopes. I see how the dark clouds linger. Full of pain & indignation. I read the paragraph—but fuller still of yearning tenderness & trust and hope. I believe, my dear love, that what you need to help on your recovery is a woman's tender, cherishing love and care, and that in that warm, genial atmosphere the spring of life will be quickened once more and flow full and strong through all its channels as of old, gradually, not quickly, even so. I dare say: but with plenty of patience; with utmost intelligent care of all conditions favourable to health, of diet, of abundant oxygen in the rooms you inhabit, of as much outdoor life as possible, of happy, cheerful companionship, & all the homely everyday domestic joys which are so helpful in their influences. America is doing what nations in all times have done towards that which is profoundly new & great, that which discredits their old ideals and offers them strange fruits & flowers from another world than that they have been content to dwell in all their lives. But for all that I do not believe the precious seed is lying dormant even now—everywhere a few in whose hearts it is treasured & yields a noble growth. Since it is

America that has produced you nourished your soul and body, she is silently, unnoticed, producing men & women who will justify you, who will understand the meaning of all and respond with a love that will quicken & exalt humanity as Christ's influence once did. Still it is inscrutable to me that the heart of America is not now passionately drawn toward the great heart that beats & glows in these Poems—that "Drum Taps," at any rate, are not as dear to her as the memory of her dead heroes, sons, brothers, husbands. It must be that they really do not reach the hands of the American people at large—that the professedly literary, cultivated class asking for nothing better than the pretty sing-song sentimentalities which "join them in their nonsense," or else slavishly prostrating their judgments before the models of the past (so perfect for their day, so wholly inadequate for ours), raise their voices so loud in newspapers & magazines as to prevent or everywhere check the circulation.

Jan. 1. The New Year has come in bleakly & keenly to the inner as well as to the outer sense, with the papers full of the details of the dark fate of the emigrant ship & of the terrible railway accidents. Percy was not able to join us at Xmas (through business) but I am expecting him to-night. My mother bears up against the cold wonderfully—& even continues to go out in her chair. Bee's letters are very bright & cheerful—she & indeed all my children enjoy the cold much, provided they have plenty of out-door exercise—above all skating, which they are now enjoying. I too like it, but am so haunted by the thought of the increased misery it brings to our hundreds of thousands of ill-fed, ill-clothed, ill-housed. I trust the family circle round you & your nieces at St. Louis & all near & dear to you are well, and that you have felt the warm grasp of many loving friends this wintry, cloudy time, my dearest—and that there may breathe out of these poor words a warm, bright glow of love and hope & unrestricted trust in the future.

A. Gilchrist.

LETTER XXVI

ANNE GILCHRIST TO WALT WHITMAN

Earls Colne, Halstead
Feb. 21, 1875.

My Dearest Friend:

I have run down to Colne for a glimpse of my dear Bee, whom I had not seen for five months, and of my Mother; & now I am alone with the latter, Beatrice taking my place at home with her brother & sister for a week or two. A wonderful evergreen my Mother continues; still able to face the keen winds & the frost daily in her Bath chair—well swathed, of course in eiderdown & flannels. Beatrice takes beautiful care of her & is happy & content with her life here, loving the country as dearly as I do & having time enough for study & reading, as well as for domestic activities, to keep her mind as busy as her body. How I do long for you to see my children, dearest Friend. I wonder if you are surrounded with any in your brother's home—young, growing, blossoming plants that gladden you. And I wonder if the winter, which I hear is so severe in America this year, tries you—whether you can yet move briskly enough to keep up the circulation—and whether you have as many dear friends round you as you had at Washington. In my walks I keep thinking of these things. Write me a little letter once more, it would do me such good. No one of all your friends so easy as I to write to because none to whom any & every little detail is so welcome, so precious—lifting a tiny corner of the great vast of space between us, giving me for a moment to feel the friendly grasp of your hand—I that long for it so. Two years are over since your illness began, or seemed to begin, dearest friend—so slow & stealthy in its approaches, so slow & stealthy in its retreat—may the spring that is coming (the birds have already caught sight of it, cold & brown & bare as the landscape still is)—may it but come laden with healing, strengthening, refreshing influences—so that you begin to feel again the joyous freedom of health, warbling once more a song of joy for lilac time. True, I know indeed, my dearest, that anyhow you are content, not grudging the price paid for your life work, but even some way or other the richer for paying it—garnering precious equivalents for pain & privation of health in your inmost soul. I cannot choose but believe this earnestly—the resplendent faith that there is not "one cause nor result lamentable, at last, in the Universe" which glows throughout the Poems is for me an exhaustless source of strength & comfort.—I see every now & then & like the more each time the Conways. I am half afraid Mr. Conway works too incessantly—that is, does not like well enough the indispensable supplement of close mental work— plenty of air & exercise, &c.,—hates walking, & indeed it is not to be wondered at in great, smoky London (I shall be fond enough & proud enough of it too when I am over the Atlantic). Unless one has a real passion for open air & the sense of sky overhead, like me. I hear Mr. Conway is coming to America for six months in October.

Feb. 25—I kept my letter till to-day that I might have the happiness of speaking to you on my birthday. See me this evening in the bright, cheerful parlour of our cottage, which stands just in the middle of the old village (it has been a village & jogged on through all change at its own sober, sleepy pace this 800 years)— my mother in her arm chair by the fire; I chatting with her & working or playing to her when she is awake; & with the Poems I love beside me, reading, musing, wondering while she dozes. Ah, shall I ever attain to the Ideal that burst upon me with such splendour of light & joy in those Poems in 1869—so filling, so possessing me, I seemed as if I had by one bound attained to that ideal—as if I were already a very twin of the soul from whom they emanated. But now I know that divine foretaste indicated what was possible for me, not what was accomplished—I know the slow growth—the standstill winters that follow the growing joyous springs & ripening summers. I believe it will take more lives than this one to reach that mountain on which I was transfigured again, never to descend more, but to start thence for new heights, fresh glories. Ah, dear friend, will you be able to have patience with me, for me?

Good-bye, my dearest.

Anne Gilchrist.

LETTER XXVII

ANNE GILCHRIST TO WALT WHITMAN

50 Marquis Rd., Camden Sq.
London,
May 18, 1875.

My Dearest Friend:

Since last I wrote to you at the beginning of April (enclosing a little photograph of that avenue just by our cottage at Colne) I have been into Wales for a fortnight to see Percy, & have looked for the first time in my life on the Atlantic—the ocean my mental eyes travel over & beyond so often and that your eyes and ears & heart have been fed by, have communed with and interpreted, as in a new tongue, to the soul of man. Looking upon that, watching the tides ebb & flow on your shores, sharing, through my beloved book, in those greatest movements you have spent alone with it—that was a new joyful experience, a fresh kind of communing with you.—I went to Wales because I felt anxious about Percy, who is not happy just now. I must not tell friends here about it (except his brother & sisters) but I am sure I may tell you, for you will listen with sympathy. He has attached himself very deeply, I think it will prove, to a girl, & she to him, whose parents welcomed him cordially to their house for a year or two & allowed plenty of intercourse till they became aware through Percy himself (who thought it right to tell the father as soon as he was fully aware of his own feelings & more than suspected

141

Norah's response to them) that there was a strong affection growing up between the two. Then they peremptorily forbade all intercourse—not because they have any objection to Percy— quite the contrary, they say; but solely and simply because he is not yet earning money enough to marry on, & they hold that a man has no right to engage a girl's affections till he can do so. As if these things could be timed to the moment the money comes in! Percy was in hopes, & so was I, that if I went down, I might get sense enough into their heads, if not kindness & sympathy into their hearts, to see that the sole effect of such arbitrary & narrow-sighted conduct would be to alienate & embitter the young people's feelings toward them, while it would make them more restless & anxious to marry without adequate means. Whereas if a reasonable amount of intercourse were allowed, it would be a happy time with them, & Norah being still so young (18), & Percy working away with all his might, doing very well for his age & sure, conscientious, thorough, capable, & well trained worker that he is (for the L. School of Mais gives a first rate scientific preparation for his profession) to be making a modest sufficiency in a year or two. Well, they were very courteous & indeed friendly to me, & I think I have won over the mother; but the father remains obdurate, & Percy feels bitterly the separation—all the more trying as they live almost within sight of each other. So Beatrice & Grace are going to spend their holidays with him this summer to cheer him up. Meanwhile, dear friend, I am on the whole happier than not about him. I liked what I saw of Norah & believe he has found a very sweet, affectionate girl of quiet, domestic nature, practical, industrious, sensible—thoroughly well to suit him, & that there is true & deep love between them—also, she took to me very much, & I feel will be quite another child to me. It is besides no little joy to me to find how Percy has confided in me in this & chooses me as the friend to whom he tells all—far from being any separation, as sometimes happens, this love of his seems to draw us closer together. Only I am very, very anxious for his sake to see him in a better berth—they would let her marry him on £300 a year; now he has only £175. He is quite competent to manage iron or copper or tin works, only he looks so young, not having yet any beard or moustache to speak of. That is the end of my long story.

This will reach you on your birthday perhaps, my dearest Friend; at any rate it must bear you a greeting of love and fond remembrance for that dear day such as my heart will send you when it actually comes: patiently waiting heart, with the fibres of love and boundless trust & joy & hope which bind me to you bedded deep, grown to be, during these long years, a very part of its immortal substance, untouchable by age or varying moods or sickness, or death itself, as I surely believe. I long more than words can tell to know how it fares with you now in health and spirit. My children are all well & growing & unfolding to my heart's content. Beatrice & Herbert deeply influenced by your Poems.

Good-bye, my dearest Friend.

A. Gilchrist.

LETTER XXVIII

_____

ANNE GILCHRIST TO WALT WHITMAN

Address
1 Torriano Gardens
Camden Road, N. W.
London

Earls Colne
Aug. 28, 1875.

My Dearest Friend:

Your letter came to me just when I most needed the comfort
of it—when I was watching and tending my dear Mother as she
gently, slowly, with but little suffering, sank to rest. There was no
sick bed to sit by—we got her up and out into the air and sunshine
for an hour or two even the day before she died—No disease, only
the stomach could not do its work any longer & for the last three
weeks she lived wholly on stimulants, suffering somewhat from
sickness. She drew her last breath very gently before daybreak
on the 15th inst., in her 90th year, which she had entered in Jan.
She looked very beautiful in death, notwithstanding her great
age—as well she might—tranquil sunset that it was of a beautiful
day—a fulfilled life—joy & delight of her father in youth (who
used to call her the apple of his eye), good wife, devoted, self-
sacrificing, wise mother—patient, courageous sufferer through
thirty years of chronic rheumatism, which, however, neutralized

144

& ceased its pains the last few years—unsurpassed, & indeed I think unsurpassable, in conscientiousness—in the strong sense of duty & perfect obedience to that highest sense—she is one of those who amply justify your large faith in women.

I do not need to tell you anything, my dearest friend— you know all—I feel your strong comforting hand—I press it very close.

I had all my children with me at the funeral.

O the comfort your dear letter was & is to me. Thinking over & over the few words you say of yourself—& what is said in the paper (so eagerly read—every word so welcome) I cannot help fancying that the return of the distressing sensations in the head must be caused by your having worked at the book—the "Two Rivulets" (I dearly like the title & the idea of bringing the Poems & Prose together so)—that you must be more patient with yourself and submit still to perfect rest—& that perhaps in regard to the stomach—you have not enough adapted your diet to the privation of exercise—that you must be more indulgent to the stomach too in the sense of giving it only the very easiest & simplest work to do. My children join their love with mine.

Your own loving

Anne.

LETTER XXIX

ANNE GILCHRIST TO WALT WHITMAN

1 Torriano Gardens
Camden Rd., Nov. 16, 1875.
London

I have been wanting the comfort of a talk with you, dearest Friend, for weeks & weeks, without being able to get leisure & tranquillity enough to do it to my heart's content—indeed, heart's content is not for me at present—but restless, eager, longing to come—& the struggle to do patiently & completely & wisely what remains for me here before I am free to obey the deep faith and love which govern me—so let me sit close beside you, my Darling—& feel your presence & take comfort & strength & serenity from it as I do, as I can when with all my heart & soul I draw close to you, realizing your living presence with all my might.—First, about Percy—things are beginning to look a little brighter for him. He is just entering upon a new engagement with some very large & successful works—the Blenavon Iron Co.—where, though his salary will not be higher at first, his opportunities of improvement will be better & he is also to be allowed to take private practice (in assaying & analyzing). The manager there believes in Science & is friendly to Percy & will give him every facility for showing what he can do, so that he hopes to prove to the Directors before long that he is worth a good salary. The parents of Norah (whom he loves) have released from their unfriendly attitude since my Beatrice has been staying with them; the two girls have attached themselves to one another & Per. has had delightful opportunities of being with Norah, & best of all, she is to return here with Beatrice (they are coming to-morrow), & Per. is to have a week's holiday & come up, so that he & Norah will be wholly together & have, I suspect, the happiest week they have yet had in their lives. Then I have stored away for them the furniture of the dear old home at Colne, & I really think that by the time '76 is out they will be able to marry. I see, and indeed I have known ever since he formed this attachment, that I must not look for him to come to America with me. But what I build upon, Dearest Friend, is that when I have been a little while in America & have made friends & had time to look about me I might hear of a good certainty for him—his excellent training at the School of Mines, large experience at Blenavon, energy, ability, & sturdy uprightness will make him a first-rate manager of works by & bye. But the leaving him so happy with his young wife will make it easier for us to part. *Nov. 26*—Beatrice has begun to work at anatomy at the School of Medicine for Women lately founded, & seems to delight in her work. She will not enter on the full course all at once—I am for taking things gently. Women have plenty of strength but it is of a different kind from men's & must work by gentler & slower means—Above all I do not like what pushes violently aside domestic duties & pleasures. The special work must combine itself with these; I am sure it can. Herby is getting on very nicely—never did student love his work better. He is eager, & by making the best use of present opportunities & advantages yet looking towards America full of cheerful hopes & sympathy. Grace is less developed in intellect but not less in character than the others. I can't describe her but send you her photograph. There is a freshness & independence of character about her—yet withal a certain waywardness & reserve. She is a good, instinctive judge of character—more influenced by it than by books—yet with a growing taste for them too. She comes to America with a gay and buoyant curiosity, declining to make up her mind about anything till she gets there. We want, as far as possible, to transplant our home bodily—to bring as much as we can of our own furniture because we have beautiful old things precious in Herby's eyes & that we are all fond of. And [by] coming straight to Philadelphia & taking a house somewhere on the outskirts of it or Camden immediately we fancy this might be practicable, but have not yet launched into the matter. I have just heard from Mr. Rossetti, and also from Mrs. Conway of her husband having seen you, & if his report be not too sanguine it is a cheering one & would comfort me much, dearest Friend. But what he says is so favourable I am afraid to believe it altogether, knowing that you would make the very best of yourself & indeed be probably at your best with the pleasure of seeing an old friend fresh from England. *Nov.* 30. And now, dear Friend, I have had a very great pleasure indeed, thanks to you—a visit from Mr. Marvin—& I hope to have another when he returns from Paris. And the account he gives of you is so cheerful—so vivid—it seems to part asunder a gloomy cloud that was brooding in my mind. And though I know that for the short hours that you feel bright & well are many long hours when you are far otherwise, still I feel sure those short hours are the earnest of perfect recovery—with a fine patience—boundless patience. And now I can picture you sitting in your favourite window, having a friendly word with passers-by—& feel quite sure that you are happy & comfortable in your surroundings. And a great deal else full of interest Mr. Marvin told me. I was loth for him to go, but one hour is so small, we have noticed, for a friend, I am sorry to say.

William Rossetti has a little girl which is a great delight to him. Miss Hillard of Brooklyn has also paid me a visit & spoken to me of you. She charmed me much—only I felt a little cross with her for giving Herby such a dismal account of his chances as an artist in America. However, we both refused to be discouraged, for after all he can send his pictures to England to be established &c., having plenty of friends who would see to it; & we are both firm in the faith that if you can only paint the really good pictures the rest will take care of itself, somehow or other—& that can be done as well in America as in England, but of course he must finish his training here.

With best love from us all, good-bye, my dearest Friend.

Anne Gilchrist.

LETTER XXX

ANNE GILCHRIST TO WALT WHITMAN

1 Torriano Gardens
Camden Rd., London
Dec. 4, 1875.

Though it is but a few days since I posted a letter, my dearest friend, I must write you again—because I cannot help it, my heart is so full—so full of love & sorrow & struggle. The day before yesterday I saw Mr. Conway's printed account of you, & instead of the cheerful report I had been told of, he speaks of your having given up hope of recovery. Those words were like a sharp knife plunged into me—they choked me with bitter tears. *Don't give up that hope* for the sake of those that so tenderly, passionately, love you—would give their lives with joy for you. Why, who knows better than you how much hope & the will have to do with it, & I know quite well that the belief does not depress you—that you are ready to accept either lot with calmness, cheerfulness, perfect faith, perhaps with equal joy. But for all that, it does you harm. Ideas always have a tendency to accomplish themselves. And what right have the Doctors to utter gloomy prophecies? The wisest of them know the best how profoundly in the dark they are as to much that goes on within us, especially in maladies like yours. O cling to life with a resolute hold, my beloved, to bless us with your presence unspeakably dear, beneficent presence—me to taste of it before so very long now—thirsting, pining, loving me. Take through these poor words of mine some breath of the tender, tender, ineffable love that fills my heart and soul and body—take of it to strengthen the very springs of your life: it is capable of that; O its cherishing warmth and joy, if it could only get to you, only fold you round close enough, would help, I know. Soon, soon as ever my boy has one to love & care for him all his own, I will come; I may not before, not if it should break my heart to stop away from you, for his welfare is my sacred charge & nearer & dearer than all to me. Verily, my God, strengthen me, comfort me, stay for me—let that have a little beginning on this dear earth which is for all eternity, which will live & grow immortally into a diviner reality than the heart of man has conceived.

I am well satisfied with Norah, dear Friend. She is very affectionate, loveable, prudent, & clear in all practical matters, well suited to Percy in tastes, &c.

Your own

Annie.

LETTER XXXI

ANNE GILCHRIST TO WALT WHITMAN

Blaenavon
Routzpool
Mon. England
Jan. 18, '76.

My Dearest Friend:

Do not think me too wilful or headstrong, but I have taken our tickets & we shall sail Aug. 30 for Philadelphia. I found if I did not come to a decision now, we could not well arrange it before next summer. And since we *have* come to a decision my mind has been quite at rest. Do not feel any anxiety or misgivings about us. I have a clear and strong conviction I am doing what is right & best for us all. After a busy anxious time I am having a week or two of rest with Percy, who I find fairly well in health & prospering in his business—indeed, he bids fair to have a large private practice as an analyst here, & is already making income enough to marry on, only there is to build the nest—& I think he will have actually to *build* it, for there seem no eligible houses—& to furnish—so that the wedding will not be till next spring or early summer. Nevertheless, with a definite goal & a definite time & the way between not so very rugged, though rather dull and lonely, I think he will be pretty cheery. This little town (of 11,000 inhabitants, all miners, smelters &c.) lies up among the hills 1100 ft. above the sea—glorious hills here, spreading, then converging, with wooded flanks, & swift brooklets leaping over stones in the hollows—the air, too, of course deliciously light & pure. I have heard through a friend of ours of Bee's fellow student who lives in Camden (Mr. Suerkrop, I think his name is) that we shall be able to get a very comfortable home with pleasant garden there for about £55 per an. I think I can manage that very well—so all I need is to hear of a comfortable lodging or boarding house (the former preferred) where we can be, avoiding hotels even while we hunt for the house. I have arranged for my goods to sail a week later than we do, so as to give us time.

Good-bye for a short while, my dearest Friend.

Anne Gilchrist.

Bee has obtained a very satisfactory account of the Women's Medical College in Philadelphia & introductions to the Head, &c.

LETTER XXXII

ANNE GILCHRIST TO WALT WHITMAN

1 Torriano Gardens
Camden Rd.
London
Feb. 25, '76.

My Dearest Friend:

I received the paper & enclosed slip Saturday week, filling me so full of emotion I could not write, for I am too bitterly impatient of mere words. Soon, very soon, I come, my darling. I am not lingering, but held yet a little while by the firm grip of conscience—this is the last spring we shall be asunder—O I passionately believe there are years in store for us, years of tranquil, tender happiness—me making your outward life serene & sweet—you making my inward life so rich—me learning, growing, loving—we shedding benign influences round us out of our happiness and fulfilled life—Hold on but a little longer for me, my Walt—I am straining every nerve to hasten the day—I have enough for us all (with the simple, unpretending ways we both love best).

Percy is battling slowly—doing as well as we could expect in the time. I think he will soon build the nest for his mate. I think he never in his heart believed I really should go to America, and so it comes as a great blow to him now. You must be very indulgent towards him for my sake, dear friend.

I am glad we know about those rascally book agents—for many of us are wanting a goodish number of copies of the new edition & it is important to understand we may have them straight from you. Rossetti is making a list of the friends & the number, so that they may all come together.

Perhaps, dearest friend, you may be having a great difficulty in getting the books out for want of funds—if so, let me help a little—show your trust in me and my love thus generously.

Your own loving

Annie.

LETTER XXXIII

ANNE GILCHRIST TO WALT WHITMAN

1 Torriano Gardens
March 11, '76.

I have had such joy this morning, my Darling—Poems of yours given in the *Daily News*—sublime Poems one of them reaching dizzy heights, filling my soul with strong delight. These prefaced by a few words, timid enough yet kindly in tone, & better than nothing. The days, the weeks, are slipping by, my beloved, bearing me swiftly, surely to you—before the beauty of the year begins to fade we shall come. The young folk too are full of bright anticipation & eagerness now, I am thankful to say; and Percy getting on with, I trust, such near & definite prospect of his happiness that he will be able to pull along cheerily towards it after we are gone, in spite of loneliness.

I expect, Darling, we must go to some little town or village ten or twenty miles short of Philadelphia till the tremendous influx of visitors to the Centennial has ceased, else we shall not be able to find a corner there.—By the bye, I feel a little sulky at your always taking a fling at the poor piano. I see I have got to try & show you it too is capable of waking deep chords in the human soul when it is the vehicle of a great master's thought & emotions—if only my poor fingers prove equal to the task! (All my heart shall go into them.) Take from my picture a long, long look of tender love and joy and faith, deathless, ever young, ever growing, ever learning, aspiring love, tender, cherishing, domestic love.

Oh, may I be full of sweet comfort for my Beloved's Soul and Body through life, through and after death.

Anne Gilchrist.

LETTER XXXIV

WALT WHITMAN TO ANNE GILCHRIST

Camden, New Jersey
March, 1876.

Dearest Friend:

To your good & comforting letter of Feb. 25th I at once answer, at least with a few lines. I have already written this morning a pretty full letter to Mr. Rossetti (to answer one just rec'd from him) & requested him to loan it you for perusal. In that I have described my situation fully & candidly.

My new edition is printed & ready. Upon receipt of your letter I sent you a set, two Vols. (by Mail, March 15) which you must have rec'd by this time. I wish you to send me word soon as they arrive.

My health, I am encouraged to think, is perhaps a shade better—certainly as well as any time of late.

I even already vaguely contemplate plans (they may never be fulfilled, but yet again they may) of changes, journeys—even of coming to London & seeing you, visiting my friends, &c. My dearest friend, *I do not approve your American trans-settlement. I see so many things here you have no idea of—the social, and almost every other kind of crudeness, meagreness, here (at least in appearance).*

Don't do anything towards it nor resolve in it nor make any move at all in it without further advice from me. If I should get well enough to voyage, we will talk about it yet in London.

You must not be uneasy about me—dearest friend, I get along much better than you think for. As to the literary situation here, my rejection by the coteries and the poverty (which is the least of my troubles), am not sure but I enjoy them all—besides, as to the latter, I am not in want.

LETTER XXXV

ANNE GILCHRIST TO WALT WHITMAN

1 Torriano Gardens
Camden Rd., London
March 30, '76.

Yesterday *was* a day for me, dearest Friend. In the morning your letter, strong, cheerful, reassuring—dear letter. In the afternoon the books. I don't know how to settle down my thoughts calmly enough to write, nor how to lay down the books (with delicate yet serviceable exterior, with inscription making me so proud, so joyous). But there are a few things I want to say to you at once in regard to our coming to America. I will not act without "further advice from you"; but as to not resolving on it, dear friend, I can't exactly obey that, for it has been my settled, steady purpose (resting on a deep, strong faith) ever since 1869. Nor do I feel discouraged or surprised at what you say of American "crudeness," &c. (of which, in truth, one hears not a little in England). I have not shut my eyes to the difficulties and trials & responsibilities (for the children's sake) of the enterprise. I am not urged on by any discontent with old England or by any adverse circumstances here which I might hope to better there: my reasons, emotions, the sources of my strength and courage for the uprooting & transplanting—all are inclosed in those two volumes that lie before me on the table. That America has brought them forth makes me want to plant some, at least, of my children on her soil. I understand & believe in & love her in & through them. They teach me to look beneath the surface & to get hints of the great future that is shaping itself out of the crude present, & I believe we shall prove to be of the right sort to plant down there.—O to talk it all over with you, dearest Friend, here in London first; I feel as if that would really be—the joy, the comfort, of that. I cannot finish this to-day but send what I have written without delay that you may know of the safe arrival of the books. With reverent, grateful love from us all.

Anne Gilchrist.

LETTER XXXVI

ANNE GILCHRIST TO WALT WHITMAN

1 Torriano Gardens
Camden Rd. London
April 21, 1876.

My Dearest Friend:

I must write again, out of a full heart. For the reading of this book, "The Two Rivulets," has filled it very full. Ever the deep inward assent, rising up strong, exultant my immortal self recognizing, responding to your immortal self. Ever the sense of dearness, the sweet, subtle perfume, pervading every page, every line, to my sense—O I cannot put into any words what I perceive nor what answering emotion pervades me, flows out towards you—sweetest, deepest, greatest experience of my life— what I was made for—surely I was made as the soil in which the precious seed of your thoughts & emotions should be planted— try to fulfil themselves in me, that I might by & bye blossom into beauty & bring forth rich fruits—immortal fruits. So no doubt other women feel, and future women will.

Do not dissuade me from coming this autumn, my dearest Friend. I have waited patiently—7 years—patiently, yet often, especially since your illness, with such painful yearning your heart would yearn towards me if you realized it—I cannot wait any longer. Nor ought I to—that would indeed be sacrificing the prudence that concerns itself with immortal things to the prudence

162

that concerns itself only with temporary ones. But, indeed, even so far as this latter is concerned, there is no sacrifice for any. It is by far the best step, for instance, I could take on Beatrice's account. She is heartily in earnest in her medical studies. I am persuaded, too, it is a splendid training for her whether or no she ever makes a money-earning profession of it. And in England women have at present no means of obtaining a complete medical education. They cannot get admission to any Hospital for the clinical part of the course. So that she is exceedingly anxious to come where it is possible for her to follow out her aims effectually. Then, I am confident she will find America congenial to her—that she is in her essential nature democratic—& that she has the intelligence, the sympathies, earnestness, affectionateness, unconventionality needed to pierce through appearances surface "crudeness" & see & love the great reality unfolding below. So I believe has Herby. Then an artist is as free as an author to work where he pleases & reaps as much from fresh and widened experiences. He does not contemplate cutting himself off from England—will exhibit here—very likely take a studio in London for a season, a couple of years hence to work among old friends & associations & so have double chance & opportunities. Then above all, dearest friend, they too see America in & through you—they too would fain be near you. Have no anxiety or misgivings for us. Let us come & be near you—& see if we are made of the right sort of stuff for transplanting to American soil. Only advise us where. If it be Philadelphia (which as far as offering facilities for Beatrice would, as far as I can learn, suit us very well). We must not come, I think, till the end of October, because of its being so full. Perhaps indeed, dearest Friend (but dare not build on it) we shall talk this over in England. If you are able to take the journey, it might, and would, be sure to do you good as well as to rejoice the hearts of English friends. But if not, if we are not able to talk over our coming, do not feel the least anxious about us. We shall light on our feet & do very well. Percy seems getting on fairly well, considering what a bad time it is in his line of business. I think he will be able to marry this autumn or following winter. I shall go and spend a month with him in July. Perhaps, indeed, if, as many are prophecying, the iron trade does not recover its old pre-eminence here, he may be glad by & bye that I have gone over to America & opened a way for him. But if he does not follow me then, if I live, I hope to spend a few months with him every three or four years, instead of as now a few weeks once a year. Anyhow we have to live widely apart. Thanks for the papers just received. Specially welcome the account of some stranger's interview with you—for me too before very long now the joy of hearing the "strong musical voice" read the "Wound Dresser" or speak.

I have happy thoughts for my companions all day long, helping me over every difficulty—strengthening me. Good-bye, dearest Friend. Love from us all.

A. Gilchrist.

LETTER XXXVII

ANNE GILCHRIST TO WALT WHITMAN

1 Torriano Gardens
Camden Rd., London
May 18, 1876.

Just a line of birthday greeting, my dearest Friend. May it find you enjoying the beautiful spring-time & the grand sights of people & products & the music at Philadelphia, notwithstanding drawbacks (but lessening drawbacks, I earnestly hope) of health, lameness. Rejoiced, too, perhaps with the sight of many dear old friends occasion has brought to your city. May all that will do you good come, my dearest Friend. And not least the sense of relief & joy in having fulfilled the great task, in the teeth of such difficulties relaunched safely, more fully, richly equipt, the ship to sail down the great ocean of Time, bearing precious, precious freight of seed to be planted in countless successions of human souls, helping forward more than even the best lovers of your poems dream, the great future of humanity. That is what I believe as surely as I believe in my own existence.

The "low star," the great star drooping low in the west, has been unusually resplendent of a night here lately & by day lilacs & the labernums wonderfully brightening dear old smoky London, constant reminders all, if I needed any, of the Poet & the Poems, so dear to me.

If I do not hear from you to the contrary I am to take our passage by one of the "States" Line of Steamers that come straight

165

to Philadelphia sailing about the 1st Sept.—& I am told one ought to secure one's cabin a couple of months or so beforehand. But if there be indeed an increasing hope of your coming here in the course of the summer, or if you think it would be best for us to go to New York (only I want to go at once where we are likely to stop, because of my furniture), let me hear as soon as may be, dear Friend. Looking at it purely as concerns the young ones, for some reasons it is very desirable to come this year & for others to wait till next. With Bee, for instance, we are both losing time & wasting money by going over another winter here when there is no complete & satisfactory medical course to be had. Then as regards dear Percy, he writes me now that though he is doing fairly well, he does not think he will be able to take a house & marry till next summer—& that I am very sorry for. But then I think that as I could not be with him nor help him forward, the balance goes down on Beatrice's side, if I am able to accomplish it.

Good-bye, my dearest Friend. Loving, tender thoughts shall I send you on the 30th. Solemn thoughts outleaping life, immortal aspirations of my soul toward your soul. The children's love too, please, dearest Friend.

Anne Gilchrist.

LETTER XXXVIII

ANNE GILCHRIST TO WALT WHITMAN

Round Hill, Northampton, Mass.
Monday, Sept., '77.

Dearest Friend:

I have had joyful news to-day! Percy's wife has a fine little boy—it was born on the 10th, and Norah got through well & is doing nicely; so I feel very happy.

Since then Per. has gone to Paris where he is to read a paper before the "Iron and Steel Institute" on the Elimination of phosphorus from Iron—which is also a little triumph of another kind for him—for the Council which accepted his paper is composed of eminent English scientists, & eminent foreign ones will hear it.—I need not tell you it is indescribably lovely here now—no doubt Kirkwood is the same—the light so brilliant, and yet soft—the rich autumn tints just beginning to appear— the temperature delicious—crisp & bracing, yet genial.

The throng of people is gone—but a few of the pleasantest of the old set remain—& a few interesting new ones have come!— among them Mrs. Dexter from Boston, who was a Miss Ticnor, daughter of the author of the book on Spanish literature—she and her husband full of interesting talk. Also Mr. Martin B——— and his wife—a fine specimen of a leading Bostonian. Besides these also a physician from Florida whom I much admire—with a beautiful firm tenor voice—very handsome & graceful too, a true southerner, I should say—(but of Scotch extraction).

Next week we go to Boston.

I went over the Lunatic Asylum here the other day & saw some strange, sad sights—some figures crouched down in attitudes of such profound dejection I shall never forget them—some very bright and talkative. It is said to be the best managed in America. Dr. Earle, who is at the head, is a man of splendid capacity for the post—a noble-looking old man (uncle of those Miss Chases you met at our house).

I can't settle to anything or think of any thing since I received Percy's letter but the baby & Norah. Love to you & to Mrs. Whitman[25] & Hattie[26] & Jessie.[27]

Good-bye, dear Friend.

Anne Gilchrist.

LETTER XXXIX

BEATRICE GILCHRIST TO WALT WHITMAN

New England Hospital
Codman Avenue
Boston Highlands

Dear Walt:

Hospital life is beginning to seem a long-accustomed life. I enjoy all the duties involved & all the human relations. Even getting up in the night is compensated for by yielding a sense of importance & independence. I sleep in a large room with three windows, & three beds in a row. Breakfast at 7, & we are supposed to have seen all our patients before breakfast, but do not keep to that rule.

After breakfast, round to count pulses & respirations, note condition, dress any wound, in charge, etc. At ½ past 8 o'clock go the rounds with the resident physician (Dr. Berlin), all the students, & superintendent of nurses. Then put up medicine, each for her own patients (about 8 in no.), give electricity, etc. If one's patient has an ache or pain, the nurse whistles for the student (my whistle is 2). She sees the patient orders what is necessary, or if serious reports to Dr. Berlin. Then there is some microscopic work, & copying out the history & daily record of the case & making out the temperature charts more than fills in the day. At 8 o'clock we all in conclave report about our patients & talk over any interesting case. One of my patients has empyema following pleurisy. I inject into her chest about a doz. of different preparations. Several of my patients (I have all the very sick just now) require very careful watching.

In the evening we go round again & count pulses & respirations & note temperatures. If a very sick patient, in the middle of the day; also take pulse, etc. The number of visits depending on the need & the competency of the nurse. I like introducing lint into wounds (such simple ones as an incised abscess of the breast) with the probe, because if I take trouble enough I can do it without hurting the patient, much to the patient's surprise.

The other day Mr. & Mrs. Marvin called to see me with Mrs. & Miss Callender—I enjoyed their visit much. To-day Mr. Marvin drove over to fetch me to lunch, & I had a beautiful drive over to Dorchester; in the afternoon a game of lawn tennis, a stroll down to the creek, & drive home by Forest Hill Cemetery & Jamaica Pond. The air was fresh after a shower & golden-tinted, & the drive through beautiful lanes & country. All were friendly & it was refreshing to emerge from the little hospital world. Mr. Marvin's cordial face greeted me when I was speaking to some patients in hammocks, under the trees, the day he called, much to my surprise.

I was to-day feeling the need of a little change of air & scene, so that the visit was most opportune.

Mr. Morse[28] is working away desperately at the bust of you; he feels as if he would get on famously if he could only catch a glimpse of you. Now might not you come to Boston on your way to Chesterfield, ride up in the open horsecars (a very pleasant ride) to see me also and give Mr. Morse the benefit of a sitting? How I wish we could get Mrs. Stafford in here; the patients get most excellent care. I have great confidence in Dr. Berlin & in the attending physician. I do not want her to come for a month, because Dr. Berlin has just gone away for a vacation.

I fear no mere visiting once a day of a doctor will do her any good—she needs hygienic treatment—massage (a woman works here every day on the patients who need rubbing & massage), feeding up (I have never yet seen a patient whom we could not make eat, appetite or not, by aid of beef-tea & milk), perfect rest, & judicious treatment.

Dr. Berlin is a learned, charming woman of 28—she takes advanced views, gives no medicine at all in some cases, & if any, few at a time, but efficient. She is perfectly unaffected, very intelligent, & has been thoroughly trained. She is a Russian.

Please give my love to Mrs. Whitman & remember me to Colonel Whitman. This afternoon, when driving with Mr. Marvin, I thought of the pleasant drives I have had with Colonel Whitman.

Yours affectionately,

Beatrice C. Gilchrist.

If it were not for records accumulating mountain high I should have time to write to my friends.

LETTER XL

ANNE GILCHRIST TO WALT WHITMAN

Sept. 3, '78.
Chesterfield, Mass.

I am half
afraid Herby has
got a malarious
place by his description.

My Dearest Friend:

I had a lingering hope—till Herby went south again—that I
should have a letter from you, in answer to mine, saying you were
coming up to see us here. In truth, it was a great disappointment
to me, his going back to Philadelphia instead of your joining us,
or him, either here or somewhere near to New York. I wonder
where that North Amboyna is that you once mentioned to me—
and what kind of a place it is. I have had a long, quiet time here,
and have enjoyed it very much—never did I breathe such sweet,
light, pure air as is always blowing freely over these rocky hills.
Rocky as they are—and their sides & ravines are strewn with
huge boulders of every conceivable size & shape—they nourish
an abundant growth of woods, and I fancy the farmers here do
a great deal better with their winter crops of lumber and bark
and maple sugar than with their summer one of grain & corn.
I expect Herby has described our neighbours to you—specially

172

Levi Bryant, the father of my hostess—a farmer who lives just opposite and has put such heart & soul and muscle & sinew into his farming that he has continued to win quite a handsome competence from this barren soil (it isn't muscle & industry only that are wanted here—but pluck and endurance) hauling his timber up & down over the snow & through the drifts, along roads that are pretty nearly vertical. I am never tired of hearing his stories (nor he of telling them) of hairbreadth escapes for him & his cattle—when the harness or the shafts have broken under the tremendous strain—& nothing but coolness & daring have got him or them out of it alive. Generally, as he sits talking, his little boy of eleven who bids fair to be like him and can now manage a team or a yoke of oxen as well as any man in the parish—and work almost as hard—sits close by him leaning his head on his father's shoulder or breast—for the rugged old fellow has a vein of great gentleness and affectionateness in him & I notice the child nestles up to him always rather than to the mother—who is all the same a very kind, amiable, good mother. Then there are neighbours of another sort up at the "Centre"— Mr. Chadwick, &c., from New York, with whom I have pleasant chats daily when I trudge up to fetch my letters—now & then I get a delightful drive or go on a blackberrying party with the folks round—I expect Giddy over to-day & we shall remain here together for about a fortnight—then back to Round Hill—where I am to meet the Miss Chase whom you may remember taking tea with & liking—then on to Boston to see dear Bee—& then to New York, where we shall meet again at last, I hope ere long. Love to Mr. & Mrs. Whitman—I enjoy her letters. Also to Hattie & Jessie—who will hear from me by & bye. With love to you, dear Friend.

Good-bye.

A. Gilchrist.

LETTER XLI

ANNE GILCHRIST TO WALT WHITMAN

Concord, Mass.
Oct. 25th.

My Dearest Friend:

The days are slipping away so pleasantly here that weeks are gone before I know it. The Concord folk are as friendly as they are intellectual, and there is really no end to the kindness received. We are rowed on the beautiful river every day that it is warm enough—a very winding river not much broader than your favourite creek—flowing sometimes through level meadows, sometimes round rocky promontories & steep wooded hills which, with their wonderful autumn tints, are like a gay flower border mirrored in the water. Never in my life have I enjoyed outdoor pleasures more—I hardly think, so much—enhanced as they are by the companionship of very lovable men and women. They lead an easy-going life here—seem to spend half their time floating about on the river—or meeting in the evening to talk & read aloud. Judge Hoar says it is a good place to live and die in, but a very bad place to make a living in. Beatrice spent one Sunday with us here. We walked to Hawthorne's old house in the morning, & in the afternoon to the "Old Manse" and to Sleepy Hollow, most beautiful of last resting places. Tuesday we go on to Boston for a week very loth to leave Concord—at least, I am!— but Giddy begins to long for city life again. And then to New

York about the 5th Nov. Herby told you, no doubt, that I spent an hour or two with Emerson—and that he looked very beautiful—and talked in a friendly, pleasant manner. A long letter from my sister in England tells me Per. looks well and happy & is so proud of his little boy—and that Norah is really a perfect wife to him—affectionate, devoted, and the best of housewives. How glad I am Herby is painting you. I wonder if you like the landscape he is working on as well as you did "Timber Creek." Miss Hillard has undertaken the charge of a young lady's education, and is very much pleased with her task. She is in a delightful family who make her quite one with them—live in the best part of New York, and pay her a handsome salary. She has the afternoons and Saturday & Sunday to herself.—Concord boasts of having been first to recognize your genius. Mr. Alcott & Mr. Sanborn say so.

Good-bye, dear Friend.

A. G.

LETTER XLII

ANNE GILCHRIST TO WALT WHITMAN

39 Somerset St.
Boston
Nov. 13, '78.

My Dearest Friend:

I feel as if I didn't a bit deserve the glorious budget you sent me yesterday, for I have been a laggard, dull correspondent of late, because, leading such an unsettled kind of life, I don't seem to have got well hold of myself. Beautiful is the title prose poem—the glimpse of the autumn cornfield: one smells the sweet fragrance, basks in the sunshine with you—tastes all the varied, subtle outdoor pleasures, just as you want us to. A lady who has just been calling on me—Miss Hillard—no relation of the odious Dr. H.—said, "Have you seen a lovely little bit about a cornfield by Walt Whitman in a New York paper?" She did not know your poems, but was so taken with this. By the bye, I am not quite American enough yet to enjoy the sound of the locusts & big grasshoppers—ours are modest little things that only make a gentle sort of whirr—not that loud brassy sound—couldn't help wishing for more birds & less insects when I was at Chesterfield—but I like our English name "ladybird" better than "ladybug". Do your children always say when they see one, as ours do, "Ladybird, ladybird, fly away home: your house is on fire, your children are flown"? But for the rest—I believe I am

176

growing a very good American; indeed, certain am I there is no more lovable people to live amongst anywhere in the world— and in this respect it has been good to give up having a home of my own here for awhile—for I have been thrown amongst many more intimately than I could have been otherwise. What you say of Herby's picture delights me, dear Friend. I have been grieving he was not with us, sharing the pleasant times we have had and enlarging his circle of friends—but after all he could not have been doing better—he must come on here by & bye.

I wonder if you are as satisfied with his portrait of you as with the landscape. I suppose he is gone on to New York to-day. I have sighed for dear little Concord many times since I came away—beautiful city as Boston is & many the interesting & kindly people I am seeing here: but the outdoor life & the entirely simple, unpretending, cordial, friendly ways of Concord & its inhabitants won my heart altogether—one of them came to see me to-day & to ask us to go and spend a couple of days with them there again before we leave & I could not say nay, though our time is short.

There are some portraits in the Art Museum here, which interested me a good deal—of Adams, Hancock, Quincy, &c.,—& of some of the women of that time—they would form an excellent nucleus of a national portrait gallery, which (together with good biographies while yet materials & recollections are fresh & abundant) would be a very interesting & important contribution to the world's history.—Tennyson's letter is a pleasure to me to see—considering his age & the imperfection of his sight through life, matters are better rather than worse with him than one could have expected. Since that was written a friend (Walter White) tells me they—the Tennysons—have taken a house in Eaton Sq., London, for the winter.

And last, not least, thanks for Mr. Burroughs's beautiful letter—that young man is indeed, as he says, like a bit out of your poems.

There are two or three fine young men boarding here, & Giddy

& I enjoy their society not a little. Love to your Brothers & Sister. I shall write soon as I am settled down in New York to her or Hattie. Love to Mrs. Stafford. And most of all to you.

Good-bye, dear friend.

A. Gilchrist.

I will send T's letter in a day or two.

LETTER XLIII

ANNE GILCHRIST TO WALT WHITMAN

112 Madison Ave.
New York
Jan. 5, '79.

My Dearest Friend:

Herby has told you of our difficulties in getting comfortable quarters here—and also that we seem now to have succeeded—not indeed in the way I most wished & hoped we had—in 19th St., taking rooms & boarding ourselves—so that we could have a friend with us when & as we pleased. It seems as if that were not practicable unless we were to furnish for ourselves. Certainly our experiences there of using another's kitchen were discouraging—it was so dirty and uncomfortable that we were glad to take refuge in a regular boarding house again before one week was out. It seems to me more difficult to get anything of a medium kind in New York than elsewhere I have been—if it isn't the best, it is very uninviting indeed. Herby is enjoying his work and companionship at the League very much. We stand the cold well—how does it suit you? Is your arm free from rheumatic pains? When you come to Mr. J. H. Johnstons, which will be very soon I hope, we shall be quite handy, and have a pretty, sunny room—a sitting room by day!—with a handsome piece of furniture which is metamorphosed into a bed at night—and a large dressing closet with hot & cold water adjoining—all very comfortable. O how wistfully do I think of one evening in Philadelphia, last winter. I shan't begin really to like New York till you come and we have had some chats together. I have news from England which makes me rather anxious. The Blaenavon Co., to which Per. is chemist, has gone into liquidation—& I don't know whether it will continue to exist—or how soon in these dull times he may find a good opening elsewhere. Should things go badly for him, either Giddy and I will return to England to share [our] home with him there, or else I want him to take into serious consideration coming out here, instead of our going back. Of course it would be a risky thing for him to do with wife & child, in these times, unless some definite opening presented itself, but I cannot help thinking that, being an expert in his profession, with first rate training & experience, and iron work & metallurgy promising here to have such enormous developments, he would be sure to do well in the end; and meanwhile we could rub on together somehow. However, we shall see. I have laid the matter before him, he & his dear little wife wrote me a very brave, cheery letter when they told me the bad news—& I shall have an answer to mine, I suppose, by the end of the month. Kate Hillard read an amusing paper on Swinburne at a meeting of the Woman's Club in Brooklyn—& we had some fine music too. For the rest, I have not yet presented any introductions here.

Have had some beautiful glimpses of the North & East River effects of the shipping at sunset, &c.—Have subscribed to the Mercantile library,—& are beginning to feel at home. Herby & Giddy had been to hear Mr. Frothingham this morning, & were much interested. Bee missed us sorely at first—but writes—when she does write, which is but seldom—pretty cheerily. Friendly remembrance to your brother & sister. I wonder where Hattie & Jessie are spending their holidays. Love from us all.

Good-bye, dear friend.

A. Gilchrist.

Had a letter from Mr. Marvin—all well—he is doing the Washington letter of a N. Eng. paper. Hopes & trusts you are really going to Washington.

LETTER XLIV

ANNE GILCHRIST TO WALT WHITMAN

112 Madison Ave.
14 Jan., '79.

Dearest Friend:

The pleasantest event since I last wrote has been a visit from Mr. Eldridge. We had a long, friendly chat that did me good. Saturday evening we went to one of Miss Booth's receptions—met Joaquin Miller there, who is just back from Europe—of course we talked of you. Mrs. Moulton too is hoping so you will come to New York during her stay here, which is to last a week or two longer. John Burroughs has just sent me a post card to say he has returned from a 3-weeks stay with his folks in Delaware Co.—that he hopes to come here soon—wants Mrs. Burroughs to come too & board for a month or so—wants also "Walt to come—& lecture"—but "Walt will not be hurried." Did I tell you that we found boarding here a young man, Mr. Arthur Holland, one of the family who were so very friendly to me & made my stay so pleasant both in Concord & Cambridge? He often comes to our room of an evening for an hour or two's chat, & by the bye, being connected with the iron trade he has been able to make some enquiries for me as to what Per's chances as a scientific metallurgist would be in this country—& I am sorry to say he thinks they would be very poor indeed. Prof. Lesley said the same thing; so it is clear I must not urge him to try the experiment, seeing he has a wife & child. Herby & Giddy both well. Love from us all.

Good bye, Dear Friend.

A. Gilchrist.

Friendly greeting to your brother & sister.

LETTER XLV

ANNE GILCHRIST TO WALT WHITMAN

112 Madison Ave.,
Jan. 27, '79.

My Dearest Friend:

Are you never coming? I do long & long to see you. I am beginning to like New York better than I did and to have pleasant times. Had some friendly chats with Kate Hillard last week, & went with her to call on Mrs. Putman Jacobi, who has a little baby 3 weeks old & is still in her room, but has got through very nicely—She talks well, doesn't she? & has a face with plenty of individuality in it. Also we went together on Saturday again to one of Miss Booth's receptions, & there met Mrs. Croly, & had the best talk about you I have had this long while. I like her cordiality—we are going to her reception on Sunday & to one at Mrs. Bigelow's Wednesday. It is true there is not much that can be called social enjoyment at these crowded receptions, but they enable you to start many acquaintanceships, some of which turn out lasting good. We had some fine harp playing & a witty recital at Miss Booth's. Miss Selous is back in America. I should not wonder if she comes on here soon. Bee is living at the Dispensary now, instead of in the Hospital, & finds the comparatively outdoor life—& the freedom from being "whistled" for all hours of the day and night as she was there—a wonderful refreshment. That coloured lady, Mrs. Wiley, whom you met once at our house, is her fellow labourer & room mate at the Dispensary. Bee likes her much. I am not sure whether you know the Gilders? We spent a couple of hours delightfully with them yesterday afternoon. She has a very attractive face, a musical voice, & such a sweet smile. They are going to Europe for a four months' holiday this spring. I admire the simple, unconventional way in which they live. Herby is working away in the best spirits. He is going to paint that bowling alley subject on a large scale. Giddy is sitting by me with her nose in the French Dictionary, working away at a novel of Balzac's. I have had scarcely any letters from England lately!— and the papers bring none but dismal tidings; nevertheless I don't believe our sun is going down yet awhile—we shall emerge from this dark crisis the better, not the worse, because compelled to grapple with the evils that have caused it, instead of passively enduring them. Please give friendly remembrance from me to your brothers & sister. Have you been at Kirkwood lately, I wonder? I suppose Timber Creek is frozen over. Good-bye, dear Friend. Write soon, or better still Come!

A. Gilchrist.

LETTER XLVI

HERBERT H. GILCHRIST TO WALT WHITMAN

New York
112 Madison Avenue
February 2nd, 1879.

Dear Darling Walt:

I read your long piece in the Philadelphia *Times* with ever so much interest, & with especial delight the delicately told bit about the dear old Pond, artistic, because so true. I know that it will please you to hear that I have gained tenfold facility with my brush since the autumn. It has agreed uncommonly well with me having enlisted under such an experienced & able painter as Chase; as a manipulator of the brush he is agreed by the experts (Eaton) to have no rival. I may yet be able to paint a head of you in *one* sitting that will do justice to you. Three of my pictures are nicely hung at the Water Colour Exhibition Academy of Design, the first time that I have exhibited in New York. We had two & three engagements every night (with one exception) last week, & go to Mrs. Croley's to-night. Your friend John Burroughs called last Wednesday—came to try Turkish baths for his malarious trouble, but it seemed to bring on his attacks of neuralgia worse. I am sorry that I can report but poorly of his health, so painfully excruciating was his neuralgia about his arms at times that a Dr. was sent for & morphia injected in his wrist, but I am glad to say he reported himself a little better. He hopes that you will come and give the lecture on Lincoln this winter; why not, confound it, it would be most interesting.

Quite often we go to Miss Booth's receptions. Saturday evening, they are gay & amusing. Met Mr. Bliss, the gentleman that talked like "a house afire" one Sunday at your house last winter, you remember.

Last Wednesday I, mother, Giddy, & Kate Hillard went to Mrs. Bigelow's reception. Miss H. was asked to recite & she recited the "Swineherd" (Anderson's) charmingly, & "The Faithful Lovers," which took every one. "Walk in" Miller was there (I can't spell his name) & lots more.

This morning being Sunday, I took my skates to the Park. The wind was high & whirled us about fantastically; ladies seated in wicker chairs were pushed rapidly along the Pond's smooth icy surface by their gentlemen escorts, tall men kissed the ice or sprawled full length on their backs, while others flew by like swallows; all this with a church spire peeping behind hills dappled with snow & sunshine: what more inspiriting than this?

And now dear Walt.

Good-bye for the present.

Herbert H. Gilchrist.

LETTER XLVII

BEATRICE GILCHRIST TO WALT WHITMAN

33 Warrenton St.
Feb. 16, 1879.

Dear Mr. Whitman:

Although not in word, I have thanked you for your letter &
papers by enjoying them thoroughly.

Down at this Dispensary we work just as hard as at the
Hospital, but our spare minutes are our own (no records to
write out); our work is under our own control; we are out in
fresh air half the day, sometimes half the night, making intimate
acquaintance with all sorts of people & places & with far distant
parts of Boston.

We have all the responsibility that it is good for young doctors
to have, i. e., in all difficult or obscure & dangerous cases we are
obliged to call in older heads & are obliged to report verbally to
the visiting physician of the month all our cases & our treatment.
Only two students live at the Dispensary—Dr. Wiley (the
coloured Philadelphia student you saw) & myself. In tastes we
have much in common & on the whole I prefer to live with her
rather than with any of the other students. We share rooms. We
have a bedroom, a drug-room, a treatment room, waiting room
for patients, & take our meals in the kitchen.

A widow woman with two children housekeeps.

I think Boston a very beautiful city. The public Gardens &

Commons in the busiest part, sloping down from the gilt domed state house on Beacon hill, threaded by paths in all directions, traversed by the business men, the fine ladies, the beggars, etc., etc. One broad, sloping path is given up to the boys who want to coast, temporary wooden bridges being thrown over the cross paths. Then, crossing South Bay to South Boston is a beautiful walk I take from one to four times a day. South Boston looks rather dingy; it is inhabited mostly by artisans & mill hands & fishermen, but walking up 3rd St., as you cross the lettered streets A, B, C, D, etc., you look down upon the harbour—on bright days bright blue, & a few sails to be seen—at sunset the colours of course are reflected gorgeously.

Somehow or other the sea looks doubly beautiful set in dingy S. Boston.

Far over in the West End too we have patients. Last Tuesday I had twins all by myself; only one, however, was born alive; the other had been dead a week. How delightful that you are feeling so much better. Shall you not be coming to Boston sometime before I leave, 1st June?

The Boston I know is not the Boston I knew in books; I am as far off from that as if I lived in England—is not the "hub"—I was reminded of that last Sunday when I had time for once to go to church & went to hear Mr. E. E. Hale preach and went home to dinner with him....

I like his daughter whom we knew in Philadelphia. She is a clever young artist. Dr. Wiley is very popular with her patients, far more so than I.

Please remember me to all the Staffords & give my especial love to Mrs. Stafford. Also to Mrs. Whitman.

Yours affectionately,

Beatrice C. Gilchrist.

LETTER XLVIII

ANNE GILCHRIST TO WALT WHITMAN

112 Madison Ave.
March 18, 1879.

My Dearest Friend:

I hope you are enjoying this splendid, sunshiny weather as much as we are—the atmosphere here is delicious. In the morning Giddy and I set at home busy with needle work, letter writing, and reading. After lunch we go out for a walk or to pay visits—and of an evening very often to receptions (but they are not half so jolly as our evenings at Philadelphia). Still we have a lively, pleasant time. I like Miss Booth very much, with her kindly, generous character and active practical mind. So I do Mrs. Croly—she is more impulsive and enthusiastic. Kate Hillard often goes with us, & she is always good company. I had a note from Edward Carpenter the other day brought by a lady who had been living near him at Sheffield—an American lady with two very fine little girls who has lately lost her husband in England and was on her way back to her parents' home in Pennsylvania— somewhere beyond Pittsburg. She is one who loves your poems, & has great hopes of seeing you in New York. She told me her little girls were so fond of Carpenter he of them—he is first rate with children. I hope you will not put off coming to New York till we are returning to Philadelphia, which will be some time in May. I find Beatrice is so anxious to get further advantages for study in England or Paris before she begins to practise, and Herby is so strongly advised by Mr. Eaton, of whose judgment & experience he thinks very highly, to study in Duron's Studio in Paris for a year, that I have made up my mind to go back, for a time at any rate, this summer; but I shall leave my furniture here, and the question of where our future home is to be, open. Herby is making great progress. I wish you could see the head of an old woman he has just painted—and I wish he had had as much power when he had such splendid chances of painting you. I cannot tell you how vividly and pleasantly Chestnut St. on a sunny day rose before me in your jottings. Love from us all. Tell your sister I often think of her & shall enjoy a chat ever so.

A. G.

LETTER XLIX

ANNE GILCHRIST TO WALT WHITMAN

112 Madison Ave.
March 26, '79.

My Dearest Friend:

It seems quite a long while since I wrote, & a *very long* while since you wrote. I am beginning to turn my thoughts Philadelphia-wards that we may have some weeks near you before we set out on fresh wanderings across the sea; and though I feel quite cheery about them, I look eagerly forward to the time beyond that when we have a fixed, final nest of our own again, where we can welcome you just when and as you please. Whichever side the Atlantic it is, you will come surely? for you belong to the one country as much as to the other. And I shall always feel that I do too. I take back with me a deep and hearty love for America—I came indeed with a good deal of that, but what I take back is different—stronger, more real. I went over to see friends in Brooklyn yesterday, & it was more lovely than I can tell you on the Ferry—in fact, it was just your poem, "Crossing Brooklyn Ferry". Herby still painting away *con amore*, & making good progress. I met Joaquin Miller at the Bigelows last week, & he was very pleasant (which isn't always the case) and said some very good things to me. Thursday we are going to lunch with Mrs. Albert Brown—perhaps you may have heard of her as Bessie Griffiths. She was a Southern lady who, when she was about 18, freed all her slaves & left herself penniless. On Sunday we take tea at Prof. Rood's of Columbia College. Kate Hillard we often see & have lively chats with. We meet also & see a good deal of General Edward Lee—a fine soldierly looking man, & I believe he distinguished himself in the war & was afterwards sent to organize the new Territory of Wyoming, & was the first governor. I wish very much that if you or your brother knew him or know anything about him, you would tell me—for reasons that I will tell you by & bye. Bee is seeing a great deal of the educated coloured people at Boston—was at the meeting of a literary club—the only white among 20 or 30 coloured ladies— likes them much.

Write soon, dear Friend.
Meanwhile, best love & good-bye.

Anne Gilchrist.

No letters from England this long while.
Please give friendly greetings from me to your brother & sister.

LETTER L

ANNE GILCHRIST TO WALT WHITMAN

Glasgow
Friday, June 20, 1879.

My Dearest Friend:

We set foot on dry land again Wednesday morning after a good passage—not a very smooth one—and not without four or five days of seasickness, but after that we really enjoyed the sea & the sky—it was mostly cloudy, but such lovely lights and shades & invigorating breezes! and as we got up into northern latitudes, daylight in the sky all night through. The last three days we had glorious scenery—sailed close in under the Giant's Causeway on the north coast of Ireland—great sort of natural ramparts & bastions or rock, wonderfully grand. Then we sailed on Lough Fozle to land a group of Irish folk at Moville—some of them old people who had not seen Ireland for forty years, and who were so happy they did not know what to do with themselves. And what with this human interest, and the first getting near land again and the rich green-and-golden gorse-covered hills & the setting sun streaming along the beautiful lough with golden light, it was a sight & a time I shall never forget. Then we entered the Firth of Clyde & sailed among the islands—mountainous Arran, level Bute—& on the other hand the green hills of Ayr, with pleasant towns nestled under them, sloping to the Clyde— this was during the night—we did not go to bed at all it was so

194

beautiful—& then came a gorgeous sunrise—& then the landing at Greenock & a short railway journey to Glasgow, the tide not serving to bring our big ship up so far. We had very pleasant (& learned withal) companions on the voyage—the Professor of Greek & of Philosophy from Harvard and a young student from Concord, all of whom we have seen since we landed and hope to see often again, especially the young student, Frank Bigelow, who is a very nice fellow. Herby enjoyed the voyage much & so did Giddy. Glasgow is a great, solidly built city, very pleasant [in] spite of smoky atmosphere—full of sturdy, rosy-cheeked people with broad Scotch accent. We have been rushing about shopping—have not yet seen Per.—shall meet him at Durham in a week's time & spend a month together there where he will be superintending your works. Meanwhile we are going to Edinburgh for a few days. I kept thinking of you on the voyage, dear friend, & wondering how you would like it—& whether you could stand being stowed away in the little box-like berth at night. I should recommend any American friend coming over to try this line—we had a fine ship—fine officers & crew—& the latter part, fine scenery. Love to your Brother & Sister & to Mr. Burroughs. Address to me for the present.

Care Percy C. Gilchrist
Blaenavon
Poutzpool
Mon.

Love from us all. I shall write soon again.

Good-bye dear Friend.

A. Gilchrist.

LETTER LI

ANNE GILCHRIST TO WALT WHITMAN

Lower Shincliffe
Durham
August 2d, '79.

Dearest Friend:

I am sitting in my room with my dear little grandson, the sweetest little fellow you ever saw, asleep beside me. Giddy and Norah (my 3d daughter) are gone into Durham to do some shopping. Bee is up in London on her way to Berne in Switzerland, where she has finally decided to complete her medical studies. Herby is, I think, staying with Eustace Conway at Hammersmith just now. He has been spending a week at Brighton with Edward Carpenter & his family—but I will leave him to tell his own news. We are lodging in this little village with its red-tiled roofs & gray stone walls, lying among wooded hills, corn fields, meadows, and collieries on the banks of the Weir, for the sake of being near Percy & his wife. He is superintending here the erection of some kilns for making the peculiar kind of basic firebricks needed in his dephosphorization process. Durham Cathedral, which was mainly built soon after the Norman conquest, is in sight, crowning a wooded hill that rises abruptly from the riverside. It looks as solid, majestic, venerable as the rocks & hills— the interior is of wonderful grandeur & beauty. When you enter one of these cathedrals you are tempted to say architecture is a lost art with us moderns so far as sublimity is concerned—except in vast engineering works. You would not dignify the Weir with the name of a river in America—it is no bigger than Timber Creek—but it winds about so capriciously through the picturesque little city as to make almost an island of the hill on which the castle & cathedral stand & to need three great solid stone bridges within a quarter of a mile of each other, & with its steep wooded sides carrying nature right into the heart of the old town. But the rainy season (we have scarcely seen the sun since we have been in England & I believe it is the same in France & Italy) and the great depression in trade, especially the coal & iron, which chiefly concerns this district, seem to cast a gloom over everything. There are whole rows of colliers' cottages in this village empty. Where they go to no one knows, but as soon as the collieries reopen they will all reappear. We often meet Colliers returning from work—they look as if they had just emerged from Hades, poor fellows—their faces black as soot—their lean, bowed legs bare—I believe the mines are hot here; they work with little on—but they are really the cleanest of all workmen, as they take a bath every night on their return before supping. The speech here is almost like a foreign tongue to any one from the south or middle of England. I wonder if you have yet read Dr. Bucke's book.[29] It is about the only thing I have read since my return. It suggests deeply interesting trains of thought.

I wonder if you are at Camden, taking your daily trips across the ferry & strolls up Chestnut St. I hardly realized till I left it how dearly I love America—great sunny land of hope and progress—or how my whole life has been enriched with the human intercourse I had there. Give my love to those of our friends whom you know & tell them not to forget us. I have had a long letter from Emma Lazarus. I suppose Hattie and Jessie are spending their holidays at Camden & that Hattie has pretty well done with school. We have been chiefly busy with needlework since we came—preparing dear Bee for Berne. I miss her sadly—had quite hoped we should have all been together at Paris this winter—but it seems the course is much longer & more arduous [there]. We spent a week in Edinburgh before we came on here. It is by far the most beautiful city I have ever seen. The journey between it and Berwick-on-Tweed lies through the richest & best cultivated farm land in Britain—the sea sparkling on one side of us & these fertile fields dotted with splendid flocks & herds—with large comfortable-looking farmhouses, & here & there an old castle; it was singularly enjoyable. How I have wished everywhere that you were with us to share the sight—and the best is that you would return home more than ever proud & rejoicing in America. It is a land where humanity is having, and is going to have, such chances as never before. Giddy sends her love. Mine also & to your brother & sister.

Good-bye, dear Friend.

A. Gilchrist.

Please write soon; I am longing for a letter.

LETTER LII[30]

WALT WHITMAN TO ANNE GILCHRIST

(Camden, New Jersey.)
(August, 1879.)

Thank you, dear friend, for your letter; how I should indeed like to see that *Cathedral*[31], I don't know which I should go for first, the Cathedral or *that baby*.[32] I write in haste, but I am determined you shall have a word, at least, promptly in response.

LETTER LIII

ANNE GILCHRIST TO WALT WHITMAN

1 Elm Villas, Elm Row, Heath St.
Hampstead, Dec. 5, '79, London, England.

My Dearest Friend:

You could not easily realize the strong emotion with which I read your last note and traced on the little map[33]—a most precious possession which I would not part with for the whole world—all your journeyings—both in youth & now. Mingled emotions! for I cannot but feel anxious about your health, & if I didn't know it was very naught to ask you questions, should beg you [to] tell me in what way your health has failed—whether it is the rheumatic & neuralgic affection that troubled you the last spring we were in Philadelphia, or whether the fatigues & excitements & the very enjoyments & full life, & burst of prophetic joy, as it were, had proved too great a strain. But you have accomplished another thing, that had to be done in your life & I exult with you—have seen the vast magnificent theatre, the free, unfettered conditions whereon humanity will enact a new drama, with the parts all so differently cast! the rest—the moving spirit of it all—hints of this, at least—flashes, glimpses, I find in your greatest poems. But, dear Friend, I think humanity moves forward [slowly] even under splendid conditions—you must give it a century or two instead of 50 years—before at least the crowning glories of a corresponding literature & art will develope themselves—Nature has got plenty of time before her, & obstinately refuses to be hurried; witness her dealings with the mere rocks & stones.

Bee is at Berne, working away merrily, rejoicing in the really splendid advantage for medical study there open to her. She mastered German so as to be able to speak & understand it—lectures & all—with ease during the two months at Wiesbaden & she has found a thoroughly comfortable home with some excellent, intelligent ladies who are fond of her & see to her bodily welfare in every possible way. I have my dear little grandson with me here—as engaging a little toddler as the sun ever shone upon—so affectionate & sweet-tempered & bright. I wish I could see him sitting on your knee. You will certainly have to come to us as soon as ever we have a comfortable home, won't you? Giddy is well & as rosy as ever. She & Herby send their love. I have seen Rossetti—he was full of enquiries & affectionate interest in all that concerns you—& loth we were to break off our conversation & hurry back—but Hampstead, the pleasantest & prettiest of all our suburbs, is terribly inaccessible & cuts us off a good deal from the intercourse with old friends I had looked forward to. It is on the top of a high hill (as high as the top of St. Pauls), & looks down on one side over the great city with its canopy of smoke, & on the other over a wide, pleasant stretch of green & fertile Middlesex—has moreover pleasant lanes, solid old houses, shaded by big elms, & other picturesque features & such an abundance of keen, fresh air this cold weather too! We sigh for the warmth of an American house indoors often & for American sunshine out of doors. Rossetti has a beautiful little group of children growing up around him—I think the eldest girl will grow up a real beauty & the boy too is a noble little fellow. I meet numbers so delighted to hear about you. I believe Addington Symonds is preparing a book which treats largely of your Poems.

Glad to hear that Brother & Sister & nieces are all well. I wish I could write to some of them, but what with needlework, an avalanche of letters, the care of my dear little man—the re-editing of my husband's life of Blake, to which there will be a considerable addition of letters newly come to light, I hardly know which way to turn. Per. & my nephew & the "Process" have made a great stride forward. Won two important law suits at Berlin, where the Bessemer ring & Krupp at their head were trying to oust them of their patent rights. Also it is practically making good way in England. So by & bye the money will begin to flow in, I suppose—but has not done so yet.

I trust, dearest Friend, this will find you safe & fairly well again at Camden, with plenty of great, happy thoughts to brood over for the winter.

Love from us all. Good-bye.

Anne Gilchrist.

LETTER LIV

ANNE GILCHRIST TO WALT WHITMAN

5 Mount Vernon
Hampstead
Jan. 25, '80.

My Dearest Friend:

Welcome was your postcard announcing recovered health &
return to Camden! May this find you safe there, well & hearty,
able to go freely to & fro on the ferries & streets. I wish one of
those old red Market Ferry cars were going to land you at our
door once more! What you would have to tell us of western
scenes & life! What teas & what evenings we would have—you
would certainly have to say "there is a point beyond which"—&
would have pretty late trips back of moonlight. Strange episode
in my life! so unlike what went before & what comes after—those
evenings in Philadelphia—yet so natural, familiar, dear! If I were
American-born, I certainly should not want to change it for any
country in the world, and if as you have dreamed—as I too have
dreamed—it is given us hereafter to have another spell of life
on this old earth, may my lot be cast there when the great time
dimly preparing is actually come. But meanwhile, dear Friend,
my work lies here: innumerable are the ties that bind us. And I
can only hope & dream that you will come & stay with us awhile
when we have a home of our own. That dear little grandson
stayed with me two months till I really didn't know how to part

203

with him, & grew more & more engaging & pretty in his ways every day—rapid indeed is the opening of the little bud at that age—between 1 & 3—& the way he had of looking up & giving you little kisses of his own accord would win anybody's heart. Bee's letters continue as cheery as ever—she is heartily enjoying work & life, and accomplishing the purpose she has set her heart upon, & the people she is with are so good and kindly, it is quite a home. She is working a good deal with the microscope. Her outdoor recreation is skating. Herby is getting on very nicely. He has had a commission to make some designs for a new kind of painted tapestry—and his figures "Audrey & Touchstone" are very much admired & have been bought by a rich American, & he has a commission for more. But the summer work he has set his heart upon is a portrait of you from all the material he brought with him—the many attempts he made there—handled with his present improved skill with the brush. I hope you will be able by & bye to send him the photograph he asked for—but no hurry. Edward Carpenter came up from Sheffield and spent an evening with us—which we all heartily enjoyed—he is a dear fellow. We talked much of you. He has been giving lectures this winter on the Lives of the Great Discoverers in Science. Carpenter knows intimately, goes freely among, a greater range & variety of men than any Englishman I know—he has a way of making himself thoroughly welcome by the firesides of mechanics & factory workers—his own kith & kin are aristocratic.

Giddy is taking singing lessons again, & hoping by the time you next see her to be able to contribute her share of the evening's pleasure. Percy is still working away indomitably at the "process," which is gaining ground rapidly on the continent, & I hope I may say slowly & surely in England. I see the Gilders now & then—indeed they are coming up to lunch with us to-morrow—Mr. Gilder[34] is the better for rest—& they seem to enjoy England; but England has done her very worst in the way of climate ever since they have been here. O I do long for a little American sunshine. We met Henry James at the Conways last

Sunday & found him one of the pleasantest of talkers. Rossetti & all your friends are well. Please give my love to your brothers & sister. Were Jessie & Hattie at home in St. Louis, I wonder, when you were there? Love from us all.

Good-bye, Dearest Friend.

A. Gilchrist.

Please give my love to John Burroughs when you write or see him.

LETTER LV

ANNE GILCHRIST TO WALT WHITMAN

Marley, Haslemere
England
Aug. 22, '80.

My Dearest Friend:

I have had all the welcome papers with accounts of your doings, and to-day a nice long letter from Mrs. Whitman, which I much enjoyed, giving me better account of your health again, & of your great enjoyment of the water travel through Canada. So I hope, spite of drawbacks, you will return to Camden for the winter quite set up in body, as well as full of delightful memories. If only we were at 22nd St. to welcome you back & talk it all over at tea! Ah, those evenings! My friends told me I looked ten years younger when I came back from America than when I went. And I am not yet quite re-acclimatized; & what with missing the sunshine & working a little too hard, was feeling quite knocked up: so Bee insisted on my coming down, or rather up, here to stay with some very kind & dear friends. The house stands all alone on a great heath-covered hill, and below & around are endless coppices, so that you step from the lawn into [a] winding wood-path, along which I wander by the hour: and from my window I look over much such a view as we had at Round Hill Hotel, Northampton, this time two years, only that with the soft haze that is so often spread over our landscape, the distant hill looks more ghostly in the moonlight. My friend is a noble, large-hearted, capable woman, who devotes all her life and energies to keeping alive an invalid husband; and he well deserves her care, for he has a beautiful nature, too, & their mutual affection is unbounded. He is just ordered by the doctors to leave the home they have made for themselves up here—which is as lovely as it can be—& to spend two years at least in Italy. So it is a sorrowful time with them—they have no children, but have adopted a little niece. Our new house is just ready & we are daily expecting our furniture from America. Herby has been working as usual, making good progress & has just done a beautiful little drawing for the new edition of his father's book. Bee, you will be glad to hear, has decided to continue her medical studies & is going to be assistant to a lady doctor at Edinburgh, who is to pay her sufficient salary to cover all remaining expenses. Meanwhile we have got her at home for a few weeks to help us through with the move in, and a sad pinch it will be to part with her again. Giddy has been paying a delightful visit to some friends of Carpenter's near Leeds—a Quaker family—the daughter very lovable & admirable. We do not forget the Staffords[35] nor they us. Mont. often sends Herby a magazine or a token. Love to them when you see them, & to Mr. & Mrs. Whitman & Hattie & Jessie & kindest remembrance to Dr. Bucke. Send me a line soon, dear Friend—I think of you continually & know that somewhere & somehow we are to meet again, & that there is a tie of love between us that time & change & death itself cannot touch.

With love,

A. Gilchrist.

LETTER LVI

HERBERT H. GILCHRIST TO WALT WHITMAN

Keats Corner, England
12 Well Road, Hampstead, London
November 30th, 1880.

My Dear Walt:

Your postcard came to hand some little time ago. I was pleased to get it, to hear of your being well, & with your friends. I have been extremely busy seeing after the new edition of my father's book;[36] the work of seeing such a richly illustrated "edition de luxe" through the press was enormous, but it is done! The binders are now doing their work, & next Tuesday the reviewers will be doing theirs—I defy them to find any fault with the book. I dare say you think it "tall" talk, but I think that it is the most perfectly gotten up book that I ever have seen. My mother has written an admirable memoir of my father at the end of the second vol.

POND MUSINGS
(Pen sketch of a butterfly)
By
WALT WHITMAN

I thought that this was to be the title of your prose volume. I will undertake the illustrations, choosing the paper (hand made), everything except the expense of reproducing, etc. I should say

London is the place to have things executed in: if you wish to give photos they must be drawn by an artist and reproduced; no photo ever looked well in a book yet! they haven't decorative importance and don't blend with type. I should suggest that we should imitate the artistic size & style of your earliest edition of "Leaves of G.," a large, thin, flat volume, a fanciful, but as inexpensive as possible, cover written in gold on blue, a waterlily say: but I could think this over. I will design fanciful tailpieces to be woven in with the text; as a frontispiece the drawing that I gave you, retouched by me, and reproduced by the Typographic Etching Company, 23 Farringdon street, London, E. C. All these are only suggestions, which I am prepared to execute in right earnest thought. I read your letter to mother with interest. We like our new house so much, & I am sure that you would. You must come and stay with us & stroll on Hampstead Heath, & ride down into London upon an omnibus & sit to some good sculptor here in London (Boem say). And you yourself could make arrangements with the publishers. With remembrance to friends,

Herbert H. Gilchrist.

LETTER LVII

ANNE GILCHRIST TO WALT WHITMAN

Keats Corner
Well Rd., Hampstead
Apr. 18, '81.

My Dearest Friend:

I have just been sauntering in our little but sunny garden which slopes to the South—surveying with much satisfaction some fruit trees—plum, green gage, pear, cherry, apple—which we have just had planted to train up against the house and fence—in which fashion fruit ripens much better with our English modicum of sunshine, besides taking no room & casting no shade over your little bit of ground—Then we have filled our large window with flowers in pots which make the room smell as delicious as a garden. Giddy is assiduous in keeping them well watered & tended.—Welcome was your postcard—with the little rain-bird's coy note in it. But I had not before heard of your illness, dear friend—the letter before, you spoke of being unusually well, as I trust you are again now, & enjoying the spring. I am well again so far as digestion &c. goes; but bronchitis asthma of a chronic kind still trouble me. My breath is so short I cannot walk, which is a privation.

I am going, at the beginning of June, to stay with Bee in Edinburgh, as she will not have any holiday or be able to come & see us this year, & much am I longing to be with her.

Have you begun to have any summer thoughts, dear Walt? And do they turn towards England, & our nest therein? Yes, I have received & have enjoyed all the papers & cuttings—dearly like what you said of Carlyle. Everyone here is speaking bitterly of the harsh judgments & sarcastic descriptions of people in the "reminiscenses." But I know that at bottom his heart was genial and good & that he wrote those in a miserable mood—& never looked at them again afterwards.

I hope you received the little memoir of my husband all right. Herby is very busy with a drawing of you—hopes that with the many sketches he made, & the vivid impress on his memory & the help of photographs, it will be good. I wish he had possessed as much power with the brush when he was in America as he has now—he is making very great progress in mastery of the technique. I observe, too, that he reads & dwells upon your poems—especially the "Walt Whitman"—with growing frequency & delight. We often say, "Won't Walt like sitting in that sunny window?" or "by that cheery open fire" or "sauntering on the heath"—& picture you here in a thousand different ways. I believe Maggie Lesley is coming from Paris, where she is studying art in good earnest, at the beginning of May, & then will come and spend a few days with us.

Welcome are American friends! The Buxton Forman's took tea with us last week & we had pleasant talk of you & of Dr. Bucke. Mrs. Forman is a sincere, sympathetic, motherly woman whom you would like.

The Rossetti's too have been to see us—we didn't think William in the best health or spirits—& his wife was not looking well either, but then another baby is just coming.

This Easter time the poorest of London working folk flock in enormous numbers to Hampstead Heath; it is a sight that would interest you—they are rougher & noisier & poorer than such folks in America—& the men more prone to get the worse for drink—but there is a good deal of fun & merriment too—the girls & boys racing about on donkeys (who have a pretty hard time of it)—plenty of merry-go-rounds—& enjoyment of the pure air & sunshine, & such sights, more than they know. The light is failing, dearest friend; so with love from us all, good-bye.

Anne Gilchrist.

Friendliest greeting to your brother & sister & to Hattie & Jessie when you write & to the Staffords.

LETTER LVIII

HERBERT H. GILCHRIST TO WALT WHITMAN

Keats Corner, Well Road
North London
Hampstead, England
June 5th, 1881, Sunday afternoon
5 P. M.

My Dear Walt:

You don't write me a letter nor take any notice of my magnificent offers concerning "Pond Musings", etc. however, I will forgive you this oft-repeated offence. I often think of you, very often of America and things generally there, and nearly always with pleasure.

My mother is away staying with Beatrice in Edinburgh city, recruiting her health, which has most sadly needed it of late. So I and Grace & a new Scotch lassie, one Margaret, who officiates as servant most efficaciously too, I can tell you (such scrubbing & cleaning as you never saw the like) we three, I say, are alone at Keats Corner; cool sitting here in our long drawing-room (hung with innumerable pictures as of yore), although it has been scorchingly hot this past month. The morning I spend sketching on Hampstead Heath, which is lovely just now, all the May-trees are in full bloom the gorse & broom are a blaze of yellow, the rooks fly constantly by a quarter of a mile (seemingly) overhead, the sly fellows giving some side like dart when you look up at them even

213

at that height. I am painting one of them; so I have to look up pretty often. In the early morning the nightingale sings, oh, so sweetly, long trills & roulades in the most accomplished manner.

Last Wednesday Miss Ellen Terry, whose name you are doubtless familiar with as being the leading actress in London, well, she called upon me to ask my advice or opinion of a drawing connected with my father's book. Ellen Terry expressed herself highly interested in our house, pictures, decorations and so forth. Her manner was a little stagey, but graceful to the extreme, and you could see peeping out of this theatric manner a kind, good heart, oh, so kind, I feel as if I would do anything for her, her manners were so winning. "Will you come to the stage entrance of the Lyceum some day soon and you shall have stalls for two; now will you come? Do." Were her last words to Grace. I called on her at Kensington last week, returning the drawing, and I was so charmed with two beautiful children of hers, a tall, fair girl, a pretty mixture of shyness and self-possession that quite won me. She too I should fancy will be a great actress some day, she has such a bright face. The boy, Master Ted, was nice too.

Well, I gave Ellen Terry a proof of a drawing that I have just completed for Dr. Bucke's book—a job I got through Buxton Forman, a great friend of Bucke's, done *con amore* on my part. This drawing has been beautifully reproduced by the new photo intaglio-process. I hope Dr. Bucke will like it, but I should not expect great things from him in that line, judging from the twopenny hapenny little pen & ink sketch by Waters which he sent over in the first instance; however, Forman rescued him from that & so far he has been guided by his friend. Whether he will when he sees my drawing, we neither of us know; but both feel to have done our best in the matter. I said that Ellen Terry must ask for you when she goes to America, which she contemplates some day. I have sold the last drawing I made in New York of you for £10. 10s to Buxton Forman ($50. odd). Church bells have just commenced chiming in the distance, a sound I like better than the parsons. I hear that the young American artists are doing capitally filling their pockets. My cousin Sidney Thomas is, or was, in America, a good deal lionized, I understand. If at any time you favour me with a letter let it be a letter and not a postcard please. I have been reading Carlyle's reminiscences—good stuff in them, brilliant touches, but dreadfully morbid, don't you think? & one shuts the book up with a feeling that in some respect one Carlyle is enough in the world: & yet in some respects a million wouldn't be too many. I often think of your remark to us one day that tolerance is the rarest quality in the world.

Interested in those Boston scraps you send my mother. You have always been pretty well received in Boston, have you not—I mean in the Emerson days? Pity that when Emerson is no more there will be no fine portrait of him in existence; there was a nobility stamped upon his face that I never saw the like of, and which should have been caught and stamped forever on canvas.

We all see something of the Formans & all like them; they have so much character, rather unusual in literary folk of the lighter sort, I fancy; but there is something very fresh and original about Forman. Nice children they have, too. Miss Blind is bringing out a volume of poems; why will people all imagine they can write poetry? William Rossetti is writing a hundred sonnets—writes one a day; one about John Brown is not bad: and many are instructive, but are in no sense poems. I am going down to tea & must not keep Grace waiting any longer.

Love to you.

Herbert H. Gilchrist.

LETTER LIX

ANNE GILCHRIST TO WALT WHITMAN

12 Well Road, Hampstead
London, Dec. 14, '81.

My Dearest Friend:

Your welcome letter to hand. I have longed for a word from you—could not write myself[37]—was stricken dumb—nay, there is nothing but silence for me still. Herby wrote to Mrs. Stafford first, thinking that so the shock would come less abruptly to you.

I heard of you at Concord in a kind long letter from Frederick Holland, with whose wife you had some conversation. Indeed all that sympathy and warm & true words of love & sorrow & highest admiration & esteem for my darling could do to comfort me I have had—and most & best from America. And many of her poor patients at Edinburgh went sobbing from the door when they heard they should see her no more.

The report of your health is comforting dear friend. Mine too is better—I am able to take walks again—though still liable to sudden attacks of difficult breathing.

Herby is working hard—has just been disappointed over a competition design which he sent in to the Royal Academy—a very poor & specious work obtaining the premium—but is no whit discouraged & has no need to be, for he is making great progress—works hard, loves his work & is of the stuff where of great painters are made, I am persuaded—so he can afford to wait. Giddy is not quite so well & strong as I could wish, but there seems nothing serious. She is working diligently at the development of her voice—& is learning German. Dr. Bucke's friend, Mr. Buxton Forman, & his wife are very warm, staunch friends of Herby's.

Please give my love to your sister, and tell her that her good letter spoke the right words to me & that I shall write before very long. Thanks for the paper, dear friend—& for those that came when I was too overwhelmed but which I have since read with deep interest—those about your visit to your birthplace. With love from us all—good-bye, dearest Friend.

A. Gilchrist.

LETTER LX

ANNE GILCHRIST TO WALT WHITMAN

12 Well Road
Jan 29, '82.

My Dearest Friend:

Your letter to Herby was a real talk with you. I don't know why I punish myself by writing to you so seldom now, for indeed to be near you, even in that way would do me good—often & often do I wish we were back in America near you. As I write this I am sitting to Herby for my portrait again—he has never satisfied himself yet: but this one seems coming on nicely—and so is the Consuelo picture. Another one he has in his mind is to be called "The tea-party," and it is to be the old group round our table in Philadelphia—you & me and dear Bee & Giddy & himself. He thinks that what with memory & photograph & the studies he made when with you, he will be able to put you & my darling on the canvas.

Giddy's voice is developing into a really fine contralto & she has the work in her to become an artist, I think & will turn out one of the tortoises who outstrip the hares. Percy and Norah are spending the winter in London (at Kensington)—and we can get round by train in half an hour; so I often see them and the dear little man. Do you remember the Miss Chases—two pleasant maiden ladies who took tea with us once in Philadelphia & talked about Sojourner Truth? One of the sisters is in London this winter & has been several times to see us. The birds are beginning to sing very sweetly here—& our room is full of the perfume of spring flowers—indoor ones. Did dear Bee tell you, in the long letter she once wrote you, how much she loved the Swiss ladies with whom she made her home while in Berne? A more tender & beautiful love and sorrow than that with which they cherish the memory of her never grew in any heart. I think you will like to see some of their letters—please return them, for they are very precious to me (the little matters they thank me for are some of dear Bee's things which I sent them for tokens). Love to your sister & brother. How are Mr. Marvin & Mr. Burroughs? Best love from us all.

Good-bye, dear Friend.

Anne Gilchrist.

LETTER LXI

ANNE GILCHRIST TO WALT WHITMAN

12 Well Road
Hampstead
May 8th, '82.

My Dearest Friend:

Herby went to David Bognes[38] about a week ago: he himself was out, but H. saw the head man, who reported that the sale of "Leaves of Grass" was progressing satisfactorily. I hope you have received, or will receive, tangible proof of the same. Bognes is a young publisher, but, I believe from what I hear, a man to be relied on. His father was the publisher of my husband's first literary venture & behaved honourably. Herby brought away for me a copy of the new edition. I like the type like that of '73, & the pale green leaf it is folded in so to speak. I find a few new friends to love—perhaps I have not yet found them all out. But you must not expect me to take kindly to any changes in the titles or arrangement of the old beloved friends. I love them too dearly—every word & *look* of them—for that. For instance, I want "Walt Whitman" instead of "Myself" at the top of the page. Also my own longing is always for a chronological arrangement, if change at all there is to be; for that at once makes biography of the best kind. What deaths, dear Friend! As for me, my heart is already gone over to the other side of the river, so that sometimes I feel a kind of rejoicing in the swelling of the ranks of the great company there. Darwin, with his splendid day's work here gently closed; Rossetti, whose brilliant genius had got entangled in a premature physical decay, so that *his* day's work was over too! In a letter to me, William, who was the best, most faithful & loving of brothers to him, says, "I doubt whether he would ever have regained that energy of body & concentration of mental resource which could have enabled him to resume work at his full & wonted power. Without these faculties at ready command my dear Gabriel would not have been himself." Edward Carpenter's father, too, is gone, but he at a ripe age without disease— sank gently.

The photographs I enclose are but poor suggestions—please give one to Mrs. Whitman with my love, or if you prefer to keep both, I will send her others. Does the idea ever come into your head, dear Friend, of spending a little time this summer or autumn in your English home at Hampstead?

Herby is well and working happily. So is Grace. Little grandson & his parents away in Worcestershire.

It is indescribably lovely spring weather here just now. A carpenter near us has a sky-lark in a cage which sings as jubilantly as if it were mounting into the sky, & is so tame that when he takes it out of the cage to wash its little claws, which are apt to get choked up with earth, in warm water, it breaks out singing in his hand! Love from us all, dearest Friend.

Good-bye.

Anne Gilchrist.

Affectionate greetings to your brother & sister & Hattie & Jessie.
Do you ever see Mr. Marvin? If so, give our love, we hope to see him one day.

LETTER LXII

ANNE GILCHRIST TO WALT WHITMAN

Keats Corner
Well Rd., Hampstead, London
Nov. 24, '82.

Dearest Friend:

You have long ere this, I hope, received Herby's letter telling of the safe arrival of the precious copy of "Specimen Days," with the portraits: it makes me very proud. Your father had a fine face too—there is something in it that takes hold of me & that seems to be a kind of natural background or substratum to the radiant sweetness of that other sacred & beloved face completing your parentage. I like heartily too the new portraits of you: they are all wanted as different aspects: but the two that remain my favourites are the portrait taken about 30 without coat of any kind, and the one you sent me in '69 next to those I love these two latest—& in some respects better, because they are the Walt I saw & had such happy hours with. The second copy of book & my lending one, has come safe—too—and the card that told of your attack of illness, & the welcome news of your recovery in the Paper; & I have been fretting with impatience at my own dumbness—but tied to as many hours a day writing as I could possibly manage, at my little book now (last night)—finished, all but proofs, so that I can take my pleasure in "Specimen Days" at last; but before doing that must have a few words with you, dearest Friend. First a gossip. Do you remember Maggie Lesley? She came to see us on her way to Paris, where she is working all alone & very earnestly to get through training as an artist—then going to start in a studio of her own in Philadelphia. She, like my mother's sister, are to me fine, lovable samples of American women—in whom, I mean, I detect, like the distinctive aroma of a flower, something special—that is American—a decisive new quality to old-world perceptions. Herby is working away still chiefly at the Consuelo picture—has got a very beautiful model to-day sitting to him. His summer work was down in Warwickshire, making sketches—& very charming ones they are, of George Eliot's native scenes— one of a garden-nook—up steep, old, worn stone steps bordered with flowers that is enticing—it will make a lovely background for a figure picture.—Giddy's voice is growing in richness & strength—& she works with all her heart, hoping one day to be a real artist vocally—in church & oratorio music. She will not have power or dramatic ability for opera—nor can I wish that she had; there are so many thorns with the roses in that path. I fear you will be a loser by Bogne's bankruptcy. Did I tell you that among our friends one of your warmest admirers is Henry Holmes, the great violinist (equal [to] Joachim some think—we among them). Per. & wife & little grandson all well. My love to brother & sister & to Hattie [&] Jessie. Good-bye, dear Walt. I hope to write more & better soon.

Anne Gilchrist.

Greetings to the Staffords.

LETTER LXIII

ANNE GILCHRIST TO WALT WHITMAN

12 Well Rd.
Hampstead
Jan. 27, '83.

It is not for want of thinking of you, dear Walt, that I write but seldom: for indeed my thoughts are chiefly occupied with you & your other self—your Poems—& with struggles to say a few words that I think want saying about them; that might help some to their birthright who now stand off, either ignorant or misapprehending.

We all go on much as usual.

Feb. 13. I wonder if you will like a true story of Lady Dilke that I heard the other day—I do: It was before her marriage. She was a handsome young heiress, a daring horsewoman, fond of hunting. There was a man, weakly & of good position, who had behaved very basely & cruelly to a young girl in her neighbourhood, & when (as is the case in England) half the county was assembled on the hunting field, Lady D. faced him & said in a voice that could be heard afar, "Sir you are a black-guard, & if these gentlemen had the right spirit in them they would horsewhip you." He looked at her with effrontery & made a mocking bow. "But," she continued, "since they won't, I will"— and she cut him across the face with her riding whip; upon which he turned and rode off the field, like a dog with his tail between his legs, & reappeared in that neighbourhood no more. She was a

224

woman much beloved—died at the birth of her first child (from too much chloroform having been given her). Her husband was heart-broken. I see you, too, are having floods. With us it pours five days out of seven, & so in Germany & France. We have made the acquaintance of Arabella Buckley, who has just written an interesting article about Darwin, whom she knew well, for the *Century*. She says his was the most entirely beautiful & perfect nature she ever came in contact with. How I wish we could have a glimpse of each other, dear Friend—half an hour talk—nay, a good long look & a hand-shake. Herby is overhead painting in his studio—such a pleasant room. How is John Burroughs? We owe him a letter & thanks for a good art. on Carlyle. Love to you, dearest friend.

Hearty remembrances to your brother & sister & Hattie & Jessie.

A. G.

LETTER LXIV

HERBERT H. GILCHRIST TO WALT WHITMAN

Keats Corner
Well Road, Hampstead, London, England
April 29th, '83.

My Dear Walt:

Your card to hand last night, with its sad account of dear Mrs. Stafford's health; but what the doctor says is cheering. I wonder, though, what the doctor would call good weather—mild spring, I suppose.

Very glad, my dear old Walt, to see your strong familiar handwriting again; it does one good, it's so individual that it is next to seeing you. Right glad to hear of your good health—had an idea that you were not so well again this winter. John Burroughs was very violent against my intaglio; on the other hand, Alma Tadema—our great painter here—liked it very much. I take violent criticism pretty philosophically, now that I see how unreliable it nearly always is. John Burroughs has got a fixed idea about your personality, and that is that the top of your head is a foot high and any portrait that doesn't develop the "dome" is no portrait.—Curious what eyes a man may have for everything except a picture. I finished lately a life-size portrait of James Simmons, J.P., a hunting (fox) squire of the old school— such a fine old fellow. My portrait represents him standing firmly, in a scarlet hunting-coat well stained with many a wet chase, his great whip tucked under his arm whilst buttoning on his left glove, white buckskin trousers in shade relieving the scarlet coat, black velvet hunting cap, dark rich blue background to qualify and cool the scarlet. I wish you could see it. Then I have painted a subject "The Good Gray Poet's Gift." I have long meant to build up something of you from my studies, adding colour. You play a prominent part in this picture—seated at table bending over a nosegay of flowers, poetizing, before presenting them to mother. I am standing up bending over the tea-pot, with the kettle, filling it up; opposite you sits Giddy; out of the window a pretty view of Cannon place, Hampstead. Mater thinks it a pretty picture and a good likeness of you, just as you used to sit at tea with us at 1729 N. 22nd St. Now I am going out for a stroll on Hampstead Heath. Have just come in from a long ramble over the Heaths—a lovely soft spring day, innumerable birds in full song. I think J. B. is right when he says that your birds are more plaintive than ours—it's nature's way of compensating us for a loss of sunshine: what would England be without the merry lark, the very embodiment of cheeriness. Are not the Carlyle & Emerson letters interesting? It seems to me to be one of the most beautiful and pathetic things in literature, C's fondness for E. But all Englishmen, I must tell you, are not grumblers like Carlyle; he stands quite alone in that quality—look at Darwin!

I should be grateful for another postcard. With all love,

Herb. Gilchrist.

LETTER LXV

ANNE GILCHRIST TO WALT WHITMAN

Keats Corner
Hampstead
May 6, '83.

Dearest Friend:

I feel as if this beautiful spring morning here in England must send you greetings through me. Our sunny little mound of garden, which runs down toward the south, is fragrant with hyacinths and wall-flowers (beautiful, tawny, reddish, yellow fellows laden with rich perfume)—and at the bottom is a big old cherry tree—one mass of snowy blossom; in a neighbour's gay garden & beyond is a distant glimpse of some tall elms just putting on their first tender green: our little breakfast room where I always sit of a morning opens with glass doors into this garden. Herby is gone with the "Sunday Tramps," of whom he is a member, for a ten or fifteen-mile walk. Said tramps are some half dozen friends & neighbours, some of them very learned professors but genial good fellows withal, who agree to spend every other Sunday morning in taking one of their long walks together—& a very good time they have. Giddy is gone to hear a lecture; our bonnie Scotch girl is roasting the beef for dinner, singing the while in the kitchen; and pussy & I are sitting very companionable & meditative in the little room before described.

You cannot think, dear friend, what a pleasure it was to have a whole big letter from you (not that I despise Postcards—they are good stop-gaps, but not the real thing). Yes, I have & prize the article on the Hebrew Scriptures. How I wish you could make up your mind to spend your summer holiday with us.

I am still struggling along, striving to say something which, if I can say it to my mind, will be useful—will clear away a little of the rubbish that hides you from men's eyes. I hear the "Eminent Women Series" is having quite a large sale in America. Good-bye. Love to Mrs. Whitman. Greetings to your brother.

Love from us all to you.

A. Gilchrist.

LETTER LXVI

ANNE GILCHRIST TO WALT WHITMAN

Keats Corner
Hampstead, Jul. 30, 1883.

My Dearest Friend:

Lazy me, that have been thinking letters to you instead of writing them! We have Dr. Bucke's book at last; could not succeed in buying one at Türbner's—I believe they all sold directly—but he has sent us one. There are some things in it I prize very highly—namely, Helen Price's "Memoranda" and Thomas A. Gere's. These I like far better than any personal reminiscences of you I have ever read & I feel much drawn to the writers of them. Also your letter to Mrs. Price from the Hospitals, dear Friend. That makes one hand-in-hand with you—then & there—& gives one a glimpse of a very beautiful friendship. But why & why did Dr. Bucke set himself to counteract that beneficient law of nature's by which the dust tends to lay itself? And carefully gathering together again all the rubbish stupid or malevolent that has been written of you, toss it up in the air again to choke and blind or disgust as many as it may?

What a curious piece of perversity to mistake this for candour & a judicial spirit.[39] Then again, how do I hate all that unmeaning, irrelevant clatter about what Rabelais or Shakespeare or the ancients & their times tolerated in the way of coarseness or plainness of speech. As if you wanted apologizing for or could be apologized for on that ground! If these poems are to be *tolerated*, I, for one, could not tolerate them. If they are not the highest lesson that has yet been taught in refinement & purity, if they do not banish all possibility of coarseness of thought & feeling, there would be nothing to be said for them. But they do: I am as sure of that as of my own existence. When will men begin to understand them?

We have had pleasant glimpses of several American friends this summer—of Kate Hillard for instance, who, by the bye narrowly escaped a bad accident just at our door—the harness broke & the cab came down on the horse & frightened him so that he bolted—struck the cab against a lamp-post (happily, else it would have been worse)—overturned them & it—but when they crawled out no worse harm was done than a few cuts from the glass—& Kate & her friend behaved very pluckily, & we had a pleasant evening together after all.

Then there was Arthur Peterson, looking much as in the old Philadelphia days: and Emma & Annie Lazarus—who, owing to some letters of introduction from James the novelist, have had a very gay time indeed—been quite lionized—and last, not least, Mr. Dalton Dorr, the curator of the Pennsylvania Museum in Fairmount Park—whom we all liked much. He is enjoying his visit here with all his heart—is a great enthusiast for our old Gothic Cathedrals, and for everything beautiful—but says there is nothing such a source of unceasing wonder & delight as riding about London & over the bridges &c. on the top of an omnibus watching the endless flow of people—it is indeed a kind of human Mississippi or Niagara.

The young folks are busy packing up to start for the seaside. Herby wants a background for a picture in which green turf & trees and all the richness of vegetation come down to the very edge of the sea and I seem to remember such a place near Lynn Regis, where I was thirty years ago, when my eldest child was born, so they are going to look it up.

We hear the heat is very tremendous in America this year. I

hope you are as well as ever able to stand it & enjoy it? I wonder where you are. Friendly greetings to Mr. & Mrs. Whitman & Hattie & Jessie & the Staffords. Love to you, dear Friend, from us all.

Anne Gilchrist.

My little book on Mary Lamb just out—will send you a copy in a day or two.

LETTER LXVII

ANNE GILCHRIST TO WALT WHITMAN

Keats Corner
Hampstead
Oct. 13, '83.

Dearest Friend:

Long & long does it seem since I have had any word or sign from you. I hope all goes well & that you have had a pleasant, refreshing summer trip somewhere. All goes on much as usual with us.

Hythe. Kent. Oct. 21. Not having felt very well the last month or two, and Giddy also seeming to need a little bracing up, we came down to this ancient town by the sea—one of the Cinque Ports—on Wednesday, and much we like it—a fine open sea—a delicious "briny odour"—and inland much that is curious and interesting—for this part of the Kentish Coast—so near to France—has innumerable old castles, forts, moats, traces everywhere of centuries of warfare and of means of defence against our great neighbour. It is a fine hilly, woody country, too, and very picturesque these gray massive ruins, many of them used now as farm houses, look.

The men of Kent are very proud of their country and are reckoned a fine race—tall, muscular, ruddy-complexioned, and often too with thick, tawny-red beards—curious how in our little island the differences of race-stock are still so discernible—keep

233

along this same coast to the west only about a couple of hundred miles & you come to such a different type—dark—blackest and Cornish men.—I get a nice letter now & then from John Burroughs. I also saw this summer two women doctors who were very kind & good friends to my darling Bee—Drs. Pope—twin sisters from Boston, whom it did me good to see. They work hard—have a good practice—& say they don't know what a day's illness means so far as they themselves are concerned. They tell me also that the women doctors are doing capital work in America—and that one of them, who was with dear Beatrice at the Penn. Med. Col., Dr. Alice Bennett, is the efficient head of the woman's department of a large lunatic asylum.

We are getting on in England too—but the field where English women doctors find the most work & the best position is India, where as the women are not allowed by their male relatives to be attended by men, the mortality was immense.—Herby has taken a better studio than our house afforded—both as to light & size—& finds the advantage great. I expect he is having a delightful walk this brilliant morning with the "Hampstead Tramps"—of whom I think I have told you. They often walk fifteen miles or so on Sunday morning.

Such a glorious afternoon it has been by the sea—sapphire colour—the air brisk & elastic, yet soft.

To-morrow Gran goes home & I shall be all alone here.—I hear of "Specimen Days" in a letter from Australia—there will be a large audience for you there some day, dear Friend.

I like what John Burroughs has been writing about Carlyle much. We have had nothing but stupidities of late about him here—but there will come a great reaction from all this abuse, I have no doubt—he did put so much gall in his ink sometimes, human nature can't be expected to take it altogether meekly. I hope you received my little book safely.

I should be a hypocrite if I pretended not to care whether you found patience to read it—for I grew to love Mary & Charles Lamb so much during my task that I want you to love them too—

& to see what a beautiful friendship was theirs with Coleridge.

How are Mr. & Mrs. Whitman and Hattie & Jessie? Send me a few words soon.

Good-bye, dearest Friend.

Ann Gilchrist.

LETTER LXVIII

ANNE GILCHRIST TO WALT WHITMAN

Keats Corner
Hampstead
April 5, '84.

My Dearest Friend:

Those few words of yours to Herby "tasted good" to us—few, but enough, seeing that we can fill out between the lines with what you have given us of yourself forever & always in your books—& that is how I comfort myself for having so few letters. But I turn many wistful thoughts toward America, and were not I & mine bound here by unseverable ties, did we not seem to grow & belong here as by a kind of natural destiny that has to be fulfilled very cheerfully, could I make America my home for the sake of being near you in body as I am in heart & soul—but Time has good things in store for us sooner or later, I doubt not. I could hardly express to you how welcome is the thought of death to me—not in the sense of any discontent with life—but as life with fresh energies & wider horizon & hand in hand again with those that are gone on first.

Herby found the little bit of gray cloth very useful—but one day *save him an old suit*. Your figure in the picture is, I think, a fair suggestion of one aspect of you; but not, could not of course be, an adequate portrait. He will never rest till he has done his best to achieve that. As soon as he can afford it (for it is a very slow business indeed for a young artist to make money in England, though when he does begin he is better paid than in America) he means to run over to see you. He says he should like always to spend his winters in New York. I say how very highly I prize that last slip you sent me, "A backward glance on my own road"? It both corroborates & explains much that I feel very deeply.—If you are seeing Mrs. Whitman, please say her letter was a pleasure & that I shall write again before very long. I feel as if this letter would never find you—be sure & let us know your whereabouts.

Remembrance & love.
Good-bye, dear Walt.

Anne Gilchrist.

LETTER LXIX

ANNE GILCHRIST TO WALT WHITMAN

Hampstead
May 2, '84.

My Dearest Friend:

Your card (your very voice & touch, drawing me across the Atlantic close beside you) was put into my hand just as I was busy copying out "With husky, haughty lips O sea" to pin into my "Leaves of Grass." I hardly think there is anything grander there. I think surely they must see that that is the very Soul of Nature uttering itself sublimely.

Who do you think came to see us on Sunday? Professor Dowden.[40] And I know not when I have set eyes on a more beautiful personality. I think you would be as much attracted towards him as I was. It was he who told me (full of enthusiasm) of the Poems in *Harper's* which I had not seen or heard of. We had a very happy two or three hours together, talking of you & looking through Blake's drawings. He is a tall man, complexion tanned & healthy, nose finely modelled, dark eyes with plenty of life & meaning in them, hair grayish—I should think he was between forty & fifty—but says his father is still a fine hale old man.

Herby disappointed again this year of getting anything into the R. Academy.

I think I like the idea of the shanty, if you have any one to take good care of you, to cook nicely, keep all neat & clean

&c. I wonder if I have ever been in Mickle St. I, still busy, still hammering away to see if I can help those that "balk" at "Leaves of Grass". Perhaps you will smile at me—at any rate it bears good fruit to me—I seem to be in a manner living with you the while.

Everything full of beauty just now here, as no doubt it is with you.

> Good-bye, dearest friend—don't forget the letter that is to come soon.
> Love from us all, love & again love from
>
> Anne Gilchrist.

LETTER LXX

ANNE GILCHRIST TO WALT WHITMAN

Keats Corner
Aug. 5, '84.

Dearest Friend:

The notion [that] one is going to write a nice long letter is fatal to writing at all. And so I mean to scribble something, somehow, a little oftener & make up in quantity for quality! For after all the great thing, the thing one wants, is to *meet*—if not in the flesh—then in the spirit. A word will do it. I am getting on—my heart is in my work—& though I have been long about it, it won't be long—but I think & hope it will be strong. Quite a sprinkling of American friends—some new ones this spring—among them Mr. & Mrs. Pennell[41] from Philadelphia—whom you know— we like them well—hope to see them again & again. Also Miss Keyse (her sister married Emerson's son) from Concord, and the Lesleys—Mary Lesley has married & gone to the West—St. Paul—has just got a little son.

How does the "little shanty" answer, I wonder? Herby has been painting some charming little bits in an old terraced garden here. I do wish you could hear Giddy sing now; I am sure her voice would "go to the right spot," as you used to say. Good-bye, dearest friend. Love from all & most from

Anne Gilchrist.

LETTER LXXI

ANNE GILCHRIST TO WALT WHITMAN

Wolverhampton
Oct. 26, '84.

Dear Walt:

I don't suppose the enclosed will give you nearly so much pleasure as it gives me. But Villiers Stanford is, I think, the best composer England has produced since the days of Purcell & Blow, and your words will be sent home to hundreds & thousands who had not before seen them. How lovely the words read as themes for great music!

I have been staying with old friends who have a house you would enjoy—it stands all alone on the top of a heath-clad hill, with miles of coppice (young woods) below it, and spread out beyond is a rich valley with more wooded hills jutting out into it—and you see the storms a long way off travelling up from the sea, and you can wander for miles & miles through the woods or over the breezy hill—or, as you sit at your window, feel yourself in the very heart of a great, beautiful solitude. Very kind, warm friends, too, they are, who leave you as free as a bird to do what you like. I have had all the papers, dear friend, & have enjoyed them.

Now I am in the heart of the "Black Country," as we call it—black with the smoke of thousands of foundries & works of all kinds—staying with Percy & his wife. Percy is having a very arduous time here starting some Steel Works—& what with his

241

men being inexperienced & times bad & the machinery not yet perfectly adjusted, he seems harassed night & day—for these things have to be kept going all night too—but I hope he will get into smoother waters soon. The little son is rosy & bright & healthy—goes to school now, which, being an only child, he enjoys mightily for the sake of the companionship of other boys.

Love from us all, dear friend.

A. Gilchrist.

Grace & Herby well & busy when I left.

LETTER LXXII

ANNE GILCHRIST TO WALT WHITMAN

Keats Corner
Hampstead
Dec. 17, '84.

Dearest Friend:

At last I have extracted a little bit of news about you from friend Carpenter, who never comes to see us and is [as] reluctant to write letters as—somebody else that I know.

That you have a comfortable, elderly couple to keep house for you was a good hearing—for "the old shanty" had risen before my eyes as somewhat lonely, & perhaps the cooking, &c., not well attended to.—There seems a curious kind of ebb and flow about the recognition of you in England—just now there are signs of the flow—of a steadily gathering great wave, one indication of which is the little pamphlet just published in Edinburgh—one of the "Round Table" Series—no doubt a copy has been sent you. If not and you would care to see it, I will send you one.

On the whole I like it (barring one or two stupidities)—at any rate, as compared with what has hitherto been written. My poor article has so far been rejected by editors—so I have laid it by for a little, to come with a fresh eye & see if I can make it in any way more likely to win a hearing—though

I often say to myself, "If they have not ears to hear you, how is it likely one can unstop their ears?" But on the other hand there is always the chance of leading some to read the Poems who had not else done so.—Percy & Norah and Archie, now grown a very sturdy active little fellow, are coming to spend Xmas with us, which is a great pleasure.

I am deep in Froude's last volumes of "Carlyle's Life in London". Folks are grumbling that they have had enough & too much of Carlyle & *his* grumblings and sarcasms. But he is an inexhaustibly interesting figure to me, & will remain so in the long run to the world, I am persuaded.

It grieves me that he should have been so cruelly unjust to himself as a husband—that remorse, those bitter self-reproaches, were undeserved, were altogether morbid: he was not only an infinitely better husband than she was wife: he was wonderfully affectionate & tender & just—& as to his temper & irritable nerves, she knew what she was about when she married him. Herby was walking through the British Museum the other day with a friend when a group, a ready-made picture, struck him—it was a young student-sculptress, a graceful girl high on a pile of boxes modelling in clay a copy of an antique statue, & standing below, looking up at her, was a young sculptor in his blouse, criticising her work with much animation & gesture; the background of the group, a part of the Elgin Marbles.

So this is what Herby is painting & I think he will make a very jolly little picture out of it. I have been much a prisoner to the house with bad colds ever since I returned from Wolverhampton, but am beginning to get out again—which puts new life into me. I have never envied anything in this world but a man's strong legs & powers of tramping, tramping, over hill & dale as long as he pleases—legs would content me and a sound breathing apparatus! I am in no hurry for wings. Giddy's voice, too, is just now eclipsed by cold.

I hope you have escaped this evil and are able to jaunt to & fro on the ferries as freely as ever.

And I hope the pleasant Quaker friends are well—and Mr. & Mrs. Whitman and Hattie & Jessie—there is a fellow student of Giddy's at the Guild Hall music school who so reminds her of Hattie.

Love from us all, dear friend. Most from me.

Anne Gilchrist.

LETTER LXXIII

ANNE GILCHRIST TO WALT WHITMAN

Keats Corner
Hampstead, England
Feb. 27, '85.

Dearest Friend:

How has the winter passed with you I wonder? Me it has imprisoned very much with bronchial & asthmatic troubles—and the four walls of the house & the ceiling seem to close in upon one's spirit as well as one's body, all too much. I hope you have been able to wend to and fro daily on the great ferry boats & enjoy the beautiful broad river & the sky & the throngs of people as of old—you are in my thoughts as constantly as ever, though I have been so silent.

Percy & his wife & the little son spent some weeks with us at Christmas & now they have taken a house quite near, into which they will be moving in a week or two. I can't tell you what a dear, affectionate, reasonable, companionable little fellow Archie is—now six years old. Perhaps you will have seen in the American papers that Sidney Thomas, the cousin with whom Percy was associated in the discovery of the Basic process, is dead—he spent his strength too freely—wore himself out at 35—he was much loved by all with whom he had to do. His mother & sister have been watching & hoping against hope & taking him to warm climates, he himself full of hope—the mind bright and active to the last—& now he is gone—& his eldest brother died only two months before him.—I cannot help grieving over public affairs too—never in my lifetime has old England been in such a bad way—no honest & capable man seemingly to take the helm—& what Carlyle was fond of describing as the attempt to guide the ship by the shouts of the bystanders on shore—the newspapers &c. prospering very ill.

A government that tries perpetually how to do it and how not to do it at the same moment! The best comfort is that I do not think there is any, the smallest sign, of deterioration in the English race; so we shall pull through somehow, after tremendous disasters.

How many things should I like to sit and chat with you about, dear Walt—above all to see you again! I could not get my article into any of the magazines I most wished. I believe it is coming out in *To-Day*. Giddy was so pleased at your sending her a paper—a very capital article too it is of Miss Kellogg.

I was interested also in a little paragraph I found about Pullman town, near Chicago, which confirmed my suspicion that it was not a thing with healthy roots—but only a benevolent despotism. I am seeing a good deal of your socialists just now—& I confess that though they mean well, I think they have less sense in their heads than any people I ever saw.

I am going to pay a little visit to those friends (friendliest of friends) who live on the lonely top of a heath-covered hill—with such an outlook, such wooded slopes and broad valleys—and the storms travelling up hours before they arrive—such sweeps of sunshine too!—& they mean to drive me about till I am quite strong again. So the next letter I write, dear Friend, shall be more cheery.

I am afraid to look back lest this one should read too grumbly to send. I don't feel grumbly however—only shut in. Herby has been working hard at getting up an exhibition here to help along our Public Library. It is so very hard to stir up anything like public spirit & unity of action in London or its suburbs—I suppose because of its vastness—& alas! also the social cliques & gentilities & snobbishnesses. Good-bye, dearest Walt, with love from all.

Anne Gilchrist.

LETTER LXXIV

ANNE GILCHRIST TO WALT WHITMAN

Hampstead
May 4, '85.

My Dearest Friend:

Delays of Editors—there is no end to them! I am promised now that the art. shall appear in the June No., & if it does I will send you at once the number of copies you name. And if it does not, I think I had best get it back & have done with the editors of *To-day* & try for some other & better opening again.

I have been reading & re-reading & pondering over Froude's 9 vols of Carlyle—"The Reminiscences," "Letters," &c. &c.— and am pretty well at boiling point with indignation against Froude—boiling point of anger & freezing point of contempt. His betrayal at every point of a sacred trust! lazy, slip-shod editing! not even taking the pains to put letters and their answers together—but printing the one in 1882 & the others three or four years after—so that half the meaning and all the *mutuality* of the letters are lost! And then the sly malignity of the comments with which they are preceded! If I live I will do my utmost to expose all this & to show that Mrs. Carlyle was no injured heroine, nor he a selfish & neglected husband. Both had their faults, but the balance of affection & tenderness was largely on his side, as well as of other great qualities: though I like her too—& think she would have scorned Froude's ignoble championship.

249

Herby has had rather better luck with his pictures this year. Has one—"The Sculptor's Lesson"—fairly well hung at the Royal Academy—where it shines out very cheerfully & holds its own modestly, I may say without maternal vanity. I think I described to you the little bit of actual life it depicts—a young girl he saw at the British Museum modelling a copy of an antique statue & young sculptor in his blouse standing below & giving her some animated criticism—a little bit of the Elgin marbles in the background. Herb. has also a little picture he calls "Midsummer"—a bit of a very old & buttressed wall hung with roses in full bloom, & Giddy's figure standing above— at the Grosvenor. Now if he has the luck to sell too! He has a commission also to paint a small portrait of me for our friends at Marley, on which he is busy just now. As soon as he has a little spare money in his pocket I think his first use of it will be a run across the Atlantic & a glimpse of you, dear Friend. Giddy is going to sing at a Soiree of socialists & revolutionary folk in general on Wednesday. Her songs are to be "The Wearing of the Green"—& "Poland Dirge" & the "Marseillaise". You will think we are getting pretty red hot! But alas! though our sympathy with the Cause—the cause of suffering millions—is warm, our faith in the wisdom & ability of those who are aspiring to be the leaders, so far as we know anything of them—is infinitesimal.

What a burst of beauty we have had during the last ten days! We look out just now on a sea of apple & pear blossoms, from the deepest pink to dazzling white—& the tenderest green intermingled with all. I hope you are able to be out nearly all day & enjoy all—and that home affairs go smoothly & comfortably & that Mrs. Davis[42] is attentive & good & every way adequate as care-taker.

I am looking forward very much to the "After Songs" and "Letters of Parting". Does the sale of "Leaves of Grass" continue pretty steady? I look forward with a sort of dread to seeing my article in proof, lest I should feel very disappointed with it.

Your loving friend,

A. Gilchrist.

Do you ever see or hear from Mr. Marvin? He is a favourite with all of us. Do you remember how we laughed at his dramatic presentation of a negro prayer meeting?

LETTER LXXV

ANNE GILCHRIST TO WALT WHITMAN

Hampstead, London
Jan. 21, 85.

My Dearest Friend:

I hope the *To-days* have come safe to hand. I am thinking a great deal about the new edition; and cannot help hoping you are going to revert to the plan of the Centennial Edition, which issued your writings in two independent volumes. May I, without being presumptuous, dear Walt, tell you how I should dearly like to see them arranged? I want "Crossing Brooklyn Ferry," "Song at Sunset," "Song of the Open Road," "Starting from Paumanok," "Carol of Words," "Carol of Occupations" and either as "As I Sat by Blue Ontario's Shore" or the Preface to edit. 55 put into "Two Rivulets"—you could make room for them that the volumes might balance in size by making them exchange places with the "Centennial Songs" and the "Memoranda During the War"; not that these are not precious to me, but I want it dearest because I want in the Two Rivulet Volume what will best prepare the reader, lift him up to the true point of view, and make him all your own, before he comes to the inner sanctuary of "Calamus" & "Walt Whitman" & "Children of Adam."

Monday morn. Your letter just to hand. It gives me deep joy, dear Friend. I have sent copies of *To-Day* to Dr. Bucke & John Burroughs but did not know of his change of address; so fear it has miscarried. I will send another,and also one to W. O'Connor.—You did not tell me about your fall—unless indeed a letter has been lost. It fills me with concern because of the difficulty it increases in getting that free out-door life that is so dear & essential to your soul & body, and because, too, I still cherished in my heart a hope that I should yet see you again— here in my own home—& now it seems next to an impossibility. Right thankful am I to hear about Mrs. Davis—that she takes good care of you—please give her a friendly greeting from me. I am going to have rather a bothersome summer—first of all, the house full of workmen to make all clean & tidy; & then my Scotch lassie, friend & factotum rather than servant, must have a holiday & go to her friends in Scotland for a month. I shall heartily welcome your friend, no need to say, & be sure to like her. Love from Grace & Herb. & most of all from me. I have plenty more to say but won't delay this.

Good-bye, dear Walt.

Anne Gilchrist.

LETTER LXXVI

ANNE GILCHRIST TO WALT WHITMAN

12 Well Rd., Hampstead, Eng.
July 20, '85.

My Dearest Friend:

A kind of anxiety has for some time past weighed upon me and upon others, I find, who love & admire you, that you do not have all the comforts you ought to have; that you are perhaps sometimes straightened for means. We have had letters from several young men, almost or quite strangers to us, asking questions on this subject; and we hoped & thought that if this were so, you would permit those who have received such priceless gifts from you to put their gratitude into some tangible shape, some "free-will offering." Hence the paragraph was put into the *Athenaeum* which I send with this, and we were proceeding to organize our forces when your paper came to hand this morning (the *Camden Post*, July 3), which seems decisively to bid us desist. Or at all events wait till we had told you of our wishes and plan. One thing would, I feel sure, give you pleasure in any case; and that is to know that there is over here a little band— perhaps indeed it is now quite a considerable one, for we had not yet had time to ascertain how considerable—who would joyfully respond to that Poem of yours, "To Rich Givers."

A friend and near neighbour of ours, Frederick Wedmore, is coming over to America this autumn, and counts much on coming to see you. He is a well-known writer on Art here—a friendly, candid, open-minded man with whom, I think, you will enjoy a talk.

I am on the lookout for Miss Smith[43]—shall indeed enjoy a talk with a special friend of yours, dear Walt. I hope she will not fail to come. Giddy is away at Haslemere. Herby just going to write for himself to you.

That is a very graphic bit in the *Post*—the portrait of Hugo, the canary & the kitten—I like to know all that—as well as to hear the talk.

My love, dear Walt.

Anne Gilchrist.

So far as can be ascertained this is the last letter. Anne Gilchrist died Nov. 29th, 1885.

Footnotes:

[1] Reprinted from the *Radical* for May, 1870.

[2] Reprinted from "Anne Gilchrist, Her Life and Writings," by her son Herbert H. Gilchrist—London, 1887.

[3] Reprinted from Horace Traubel's "With Walt Whitman in Camden," I, 219-220. Although addressed to Rossetti, this letter is evidently intended as much for Mrs. Gilchrist, whose name was not at this time known to Whitman.

[4] Alexander Gilchrist.

[5] Mrs. Gilchrist's emotion here apparently prevents her memory from doing complete justice to her own past. For a very different expression of her feelings toward Alexander Gilchrist, written

at the time of her betrothal, see her letter announcing the engagement which she sent to her friend, Julia Newton, and which is to be found on pp. 30-31 of her son's biography.

[6] William Michael Rossetti.

[7] To W. M. Rossetti. See *ante*, p. x.

[8] First printed in Horace Traubel's "With Walt Whitman in Camden," III, 513.

[9] Evidently meaning the letter of September 3d.

[10] Missing.

[11] Percy Carlyle Gilchrist who became an inventive metallurgist.

[12] Herbert Harlakenden Gilchrist, who became an artist.

[13] Printed from copy retained by Whitman.

[14] To deliver his Dartmouth College ode.

[15] William Douglas O'Connor, an ardent Washington friend of Whitman.

[16] John Burroughs, the naturalist, then a young author and disciple of Whitman.

[17] Anne Gilchrist's son.

[18] Horace Greeley, nominated by the Democrats as their candidate for the Presidency.

[19] Burlington, Vermont, where Whitman's sister, Mrs. Heyde, lived.

[20] Henry M. Stanley, African Explorer.

[21] Undated. Made up from copy among Whitman's papers. This letter evidently belongs to the summer of 1873.

[22] The "Prayer of Columbus" was first published in *Harper's Magazine* in March, 1874.

[23] John Cowardine. See "Anne Gilchrist, Her Life and Writings," pp. 149 ff.

[24] Daughters of Thomas Jefferson Whitman.

[25] Mrs. George Whitman.

[26] Sister.

[27] Niece.

[28] Sidney Morse, the sculptor.

[29] "Man's Moral Nature," by Dr. Richard Maurice Bucke.

[30] This extract (?) is taken from H. H. Gilchrist's "Anne Gilchrist,"

p. 252. It is undated, but it is clearly a reply to the foregoing letter from Mrs. Gilchrist.

[31] Durham Cathedral.

[32] Anne Gilchrist's grandchild.

[33] Reproduced in "Anne Gilchrist, Her Life and Writings," facing p. 253.

[34] Richard Watson Gilder.

[35] Of Timber Creek, Camden County, New Jersey, whose hospitality helped Whitman to improve his health.

[36] The second edition of Alexander Gilchrist's "William Blake."

[37] Because of the death of her daughter Beatrice.

[38] Whitman's London publisher.

[39] Dr. Bucke, in his "Life of Whitman," had reprinted at the end of the volume many criticisms of the poet, adverse as well as favourable; likewise W. D. O'Connor's "Good Gray Poet."

[40] Edward Dowden, of the University of Dublin.

[41] Artists, famous for their etchings. Mr. Pennell made several etchings for Dr. Bucke's biography of Whitman.

[42] Mrs. Mary Davis, who was Whitman's housekeeper until his death.

[43] Daughter of Pearsall Smith, of Philadelphia.

Lightning Source UK Ltd.
Milton Keynes UK
UKHW012142171221
395843UK00002B/575